Landmarks of world literature

Goethe

THE SORROWS OF YOUNG WERTHER

Landmarks of world literature

General Editor: J. P. Stern

GOETHE

The Sorrows of
Young Werther

MARTIN SWALES

Department of German,
University College, London

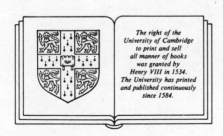

The right of the
University of Cambridge
to print and sell
all manner of books
was granted by
Henry VIII in 1534.
The University has printed
and published continuously
since 1584.

CAMBRIDGE UNIVERSITY PRESS

Cambridge
New York   New Rochelle   Melbourne   Sydney

Published by the Press Syndicate of the University of Cambridge
The Pitt Building, Trumpington Street, Cambridge CB2 1RP
32 East 57th Street, New York, NY 10022, USA
10 Stamford Road, Oakleigh, Melbourne 3166, Australia

© Cambridge University Press 1987

First published 1987

Printed in Great Britain at
the University Press, Cambridge

British Library cataloguing in publication data

Swales, Martin
Goethe: The sorrows of young Werther. –
(Landmarks of world literature).
1. Goethe, Johann Wolfgang von
I. Title   II. Series
833′.6   PT1980

Library of Congress cataloguing in publication data

Swales, Martin.
Goethe: the sorrows of young Werther.
(Landmarks of world literature)
Bibliography.
1. Goethe, Johann Wolfgang von, 1749–1832. Werther.
I. Title.   II. Series.
PT1980.S93   1987   833′.6   87–11757

ISBN 0 521 32818 7 hard covers
ISBN 0 521 31699 5 paperback

VN

Contents

Preface

The tradition of the German novel, before the emergence of its 'classic' writers in the first half of the twentieth century (Thomas Mann, Kafka, Hesse, Musil), does not have an assured place in the canon of European literature. Not that it has wanted for spirited advocates; but, despite all efforts, it has remained firmly on the periphery. The one signal exception is Goethe's novel *Die Leiden des jungen Werthers* (as the title was given in the first edition) or (as most subsequent printings have it) *Die Leiden des jungen Werther*. The title (with or without the genitive form ending in '–s') is usually rendered as 'The Sorrows of Young Werther' – and I shall have a word to say about that translation in the main text. *Werther* was an extraordinary and immediate bestseller both in Germany and abroad. For this reason, one does not have to plead for its importance: it is, as it were, already on the map. But even so, it does pose interpretative problems for us as modern readers. There is, for example, the fact that *Werther* was, as I shall show, very much rooted in contemporary taste: and it may be that some modern readers will find that they can only view it as a quaint museum piece. This has not been my experience in teaching the novel. My students at University College London have found *Werther* an exciting and troubling text – one that produces strongly divergent opinions. I am grateful to them for the enthusiasm and energy with which they have discussed this novel: their contribution to the making of this title in the *Landmarks of world literature* series has been decisive, as has that of my colleague and friend Peter Stern.

The translations given are my own. Because Werther's letters are, for the most part, carefully dated, I have been able to give as the source for any particular quotation the date of the letter from which it comes. Where I have quoted from the editor's narrative, I have always attempted to give a clear indication of where the passage is to be found.

My debt to other critics is acknowledged in the 'Guide to further reading' which forms the last part of this book.

MARTIN SWALES

University College London

vii

Chronology

	Goethe's life and work	Contemporary events
1740		Richardson, *Pamela*
1742–5		Young, *Night Thoughts*
1748		First three cantos of Klopstock's *Der Messias* published; Montesquieu, *L'Esprit des Lois*;
1741–8		Richardson, *Clarissa Harlowe*; Voltaire, *Zadig*.
1749	28 August: Goethe born in Frankfurt on the Main	War of the Austrian Succession
1756–63		Seven Years War
1759		Voltaire, *Candide*
1760		First two volumes of Sterne's *Tristram Shandy* published
1760–3		Ossian
1761		Rousseau, *La nouvelle Héloïse*
1762		Rousseau, *Le Contrat social*, *Émile*
1765–8	Law studies in Leipzig	
1766		Goldsmith, *The Vicar of Wakefield*
1767		Lessing, *Minna von Barnhelm*
1768		Sterne, *Sentimental Journey*
1770	Love affair with Friederike Brion at Sesenheim. Early poems ('Willkommen und Abschied', 'Mailied')	

1771	Translates Ossian. *Rede zum Schäkespears Tag*	Klopstock, *Oden*; Smollett, *Humphry Clinker*
1772	*Von deutscher Baukunst*. Period spent at Wetzlar ('Reichskammergericht'), love for Charlotte Buff	Lessing, *Emilia Galotti*
1772–3	Meetings with Maximiliane von La Roche (later Brentano)	
1773	*Götz von Berlichingen*	
1774	*Die Leiden des jungen Werthers*, first version; *Clavigo*	
1775	Engagement to Lili Schönemann (but broken off in September). Invited to Weimar by Duke Karl August. Arrives Weimar 7 November. Begins work on *Egmont*	Beaumarchais, *Le Barbier de Séville*; Sheridan, *The Rivals*
1775–83	Settles in Weimar, takes up official duties, studies botany and geology. Begins work on *Wilhelm Meister*	American War of Independence
1776		American Declaration of Independence; Lenz, *Die Soldaten*
1776–88	Relationship with Charlotte von Stein	
1778		Death of Voltaire and Rousseau
1779	Appointed 'geheimer Rat' (privy counsellor)	Lessing, *Nathan der Weise*
1781		Schiller, *Die Räuber*; Kant, *Kritik der reinen Vernunft*
1782	Given patent of nobility	Laclos, *Les Liaisons dangereuses*
1784	Scientific work – discovery of intermaxillary bone in animal and human jaw. Essay *Über den Granit*	Schiller, *Kabale und Liebe*; Herder, *Ideen zu einer Philosophie der Geschichte der Menschheit*; Beaumarchais, *Le Mariage de Figaro*
1786–8	Italian journey. Sudden, secret departure from Weimar via Karlsbad, 3 September 1786.	
1786		Mozart, *The Marriage of Figaro*. Death of Frederick the Great

	Goethe's life and work	Contemporary events
1787	Visits Naples and Sicily. *Die Leiden des jungen Werther*, second version. *Iphigenie auf Tauris*	Schiller, *Don Carlos*; Mozart, *Don Giovanni*
1788	*Egmont*. Continues work on *Faust*, *Torquato Tasso*, *Wilhelm Meister*. Returns to Weimar in June. Relationship with Christiane Vulpius, break with Charlotte von Stein.	Kant, *Kritik der praktischen Vernunft*
1788–1806	Studies of morphology and optics.	
1789	*Torquato Tasso* completed (published in 1790). Birth of son, August	Storming of the Bastille. Blake, *Songs of Innocence*
1789–91		Constituent Assembly in France
1790	*Faust, ein Fragment*, *Über die Metamorphose der Pflanzen*	
1791	Assumes charge of Weimar theatre (till 1817)	
1792–3	Takes part with the Duke in campaign against revolutionaries in France. *Die Campagne in Frankreich*	
1793		Execution of Louis XVI. Reign of Terror in France
1794	Beginning of friendship with Schiller (which lasts until the latter's death in 1805)	
1795–6	*Wilhelm Meisters Lehrjahre*	
1795		Schiller, *Briefe über die ästhetische Erziehung*
1796		Napoleon's campaign in Italy
1797–9		Hölderlin, *Hyperion*
1797	*Hermann und Dorothea*	

1798	*Balladenalmanach*	Wordsworth and Coleridge, *Lyrical Ballads*
1799		Friedrich Schlegel, *Lucinde*
1800		Schiller, *Maria Stuart*; Novalis, *Hymnen an die Nacht*; Mme de Staël, *De la Littérature*
1801		Schiller, *Die Jungfrau von Orleans*;
1802		Chateaubriand, *Atala*
1804		Novalis. *Heinrich von Ofterdingen* / Napoleon crowned Emperor. Schiller, *Wilhelm Tell*
1805		Battle of Trafalgar. Chateaubriand, *René*. Death of Schiller
1806	*Faust. Part One* completed (published 1808).	Dissolution of Holy Roman Empire. Battle of Jena (defeat of Prussia and Austria)
1807	Marries Christiane Vulpius / Begins work on *Die Wahlverwandtschaften* (published 1809)	
1808	Meeting with Napoleon at Erfurt	Kleist, *Penthesilea*
1808–31	Works on autobiography *Dichtung und Wahrheit*	
1810		Kleist, *Prinz Friedrich von Homburg*; Mme de Staël, *De l'Allemagne*
1811		Jane Austen, *Sense and Sensibility*
1812		Napoleon's retreat from Moscow. Byron, *Childe Harold*
1814		Scott, *Waverley*; Wordsworth, *The Excursion*; E. T. A. Hoffmann, *Fantasiestücke in Callots Manier*
1814–15	Journeys to Rhine and Main, love for Marianne von Willemer. Begins work on *Der West-Östliche Divan*	

	Goethe's life and work	Contemporary events
1815		The Hundred Days, Napoleon defeated at Waterloo
1816	Death of Christiane	Coleridge, *Kubla Khan*; Constant, *Adolphe*
1817		Keats, *Poems*; Byron, *Don Juan*
1818		Mary Shelley, *Frankenstein*
1819		Schopenhauer, *Die Welt als Wille und Vorstellung*
1820		Lamartine, *Premières Méditations*; Shelley, *Prometheus Unbound*
1822		Heine, *Gedichte*, Vigny, *Poèmes*
1823	Begins conversations with Eckermann. Love for Ulrike von Levetzow, writes 'Marienbader Elegie'	
1824	Writes 'An Werther'. Takes up work on *Faust. Part Two*, which will occupy him till 1831	
1825		Grillparzer, *König Ottokars Glück und Ende*
1826	*Novelle*	Eichendorff, *Aus dem Leben eines Taugenichts*; Victor Hugo, *Odes et Ballades*
1827	Death of Charlotte von Stein	Hugo, *Préface de 'Cromwell'*
1828	Death of Karl August	
1829	*Wilhelm Meisters Wanderjahre*	Balzac, *Les Chouans*; Musset, *Poésies*; Hugo, *Les Orientales*
1830		July revolution in France. Hugo, *Hernani*; Tennyson, *Poems*
1831	*Dichtung und Wahrheit* completed, *Faust. Part Two* completed (published posthumously, 1832)	Stendhal, *Le Rouge et le Noir*; Hugo, *Notre-Dame de Paris*
1832	Goethe dies, 22 March	

Chapter 1

Werther in context

(a) Territories and nationhood

Goethe's novel *The Sorrows of Young Werther*, which first appeared in 1774 (to be followed by a second version in 1787), was an immediate success: not only was it a bestseller in Germany, in the space of a few years it captured the imagination of European readers as well. One of the aims of this study is to explain why and how *Werther* had this colossal impact. The international success it achieved becomes all the more remarkable when we remember that it emerged from a country that was different in kind from the other European nations. The particularity (in a variety of senses) of Germany has been – and still is – an issue within European historiography.

Historians employ a number of terms to characterize the course of German history prior to 1871. Notions such as 'der deutsche Sonderweg' (the special course of Germany) or 'die verspätete Nation' (the belated nation) recur constantly. They express the idea that the German lands constituted an exception to the (European) historical norm in that Germany only became a unified nation state three decades from the end of the nineteenth century. Before then 'Germany' existed only as a cultural entity defined by a shared language, and not as a political unit. The Holy Roman Empire administered a complex system of rights and privileges which provided a loose administrative and judicial framework within which a profusion of large and small territories could operate (rather than co-operate). Its prevailing ethos allowed a large measure of autonomy to its constituent territories, and that autonomy expressed itself as princely absolutism. This conglomeration of small, largely independent states ('Kleinstaaterei') became more centrifugal after the Thirty Years War. The settlements of Westphalia, which concluded that war in 1648, permitted the protection of 'German liberties' by non-German powers: in practice this meant that German princes had the freedom to make alliances which further undermined the Empire's role as a unifying force. And this process of political weakening came hard on the heels of the appalling destruction which the war had brought to whole areas of Germany: estimates indicate that the German lands lost some 40 per cent of their rural and 33 per cent of their urban population in the war. Economically, the recovery was slow in coming; and it was not helped by the particularism that generated a bewildering array of currencies and tariff barriers. For the year 1780 the Worms register lists 314 imperial territories and, for the most part, their allegiance to the Emperor was little more than nominal. Administratively, the Empire functioned through three principal institutions: the Imperial Assembly ('Reichstag') at Regensburg, the Supreme Court ('Reichskammergericht') which had met at Speyer until 1684 but then moved to Wetzlar, and the Imperial Tribunal ('Reichshofrat') in Vienna.

It is all too tempting to be dismissive of the Holy Roman Empire, to see it as a ponderous machine which delayed the attainment of German national unity; and to argue that, when that unity finally came, it was so radically out of synchrony with the rapid transformation of late nineteenth-century Germany into an industrial nation that the seeds of catastrophe were already sown. But this is to subscribe to the view which, in hindsight, invests German history from late medieval times to the first decades of the twentieth century with a kind of inbuilt pathology. The Empire may have a number of things to answer for. But to make it responsible for everything, down to and including Hitler, is excessive. Certainly many of the petty rulers in the German lands were tyrants; certainly the administrative institutions of the Empire were ponderous (the Supreme Court was woefully underfunded and could not keep up with the volume of work – Goethe in the twelfth book of his auto-biography *Poetry and Truth* speaks of some twenty thousand cases being before the Wetzlar authorities, of which only sixty could be dealt with in any year); certainly political docility was inculcated into German citizens, and many were content to see freedom as an inward, spiritual entity, as something different from (and, indeed, preferable to) the mundane and outward thing known as political liberty. This brings us to the key notion of inwardness ('Innerlichkeit') which has so often been seen as the besetting sin of the German nation. It is pilloried by Karl Marx with his notion of the 'deutsche Misere'. Behind such arguments, persuasive though they may be, there lurks a kind of (often unspoken) normative thinking: one which decrees that the 'healthy' course of a European nation's political, social, and economic development from the eighteenth to the twentieth century is synonymous with the cumulative self-assertion of the bourgeois class as a motor force for radical social change within the unified nation state.

It can readily be admitted that neither the Holy Roman Empire nor the German Confederation which succeeded it in the nineteenth century accord with such a norm (the 1848 revolution, which promised a measure of political reform, came to nothing). But this does not mean that the Empire and its legacy are to be identified as some malignant growth on the body of European history. The Empire did, after all, enable small, virtually unprotected territories to survive alongside powerful states. Moreover, as the German lands slowly recovered from the consequences of the Thirty Years War, enlightened and progressive energies made themselves felt – even within the essentially absolutist context. However strange it may sound to modern ears, one vital agency of this enlightened thinking was the bureaucracy which sprang up at the various courts. From the second half of the seventeenth century on, many princes were concerned to promote economic and social stability in their domains, and this aim brought with it the need for people with administrative skills. Of course, at the courts the power and prestige of the nobility remained largely unbroken. But for their efficient running the territories depended on new generations of (usually university-trained) administrators, and the civil service began to acquire for itself a measure of influence and respect. The need for academically trained people produced a veneration for the institutions of learning (both school and university). Universities, academies, botanical gardens, libraries, reading circles, scientific 'cabinets' flourished. And they all opened the way for bourgeois self-advancement. Journalism too acquired a new energy: the eighteenth century witnessed the growth of the moral weeklies ('moralische Wochenschriften'), in which ethical issues were discussed – often in a form that mixed narrative (anecdote) with debate. Admittedly, eighteenth-century Germany has no equivalent of the lively civic atmosphere, the coffee houses, the vigorous journals, pamphlets, and newspapers of contemporary London: such a capital city exuded a degree of self-assurance and disputative sophistication which could scarcely arise in the loose aggregation of territories that was Germany. But even so, it would be a mistake to see the German-speaking lands as belonging to a different planet.

Werther is not a novel that, in any obvious, sustained, or exacting way, takes issue with the society of its time. It tells the story of a young man of great sensitivity, who is sent by his mother on a journey to a small town where he is to clarify the matter of an outstanding legacy. He is enchanted by the beauty of his surroundings. After a few weeks he meets, and falls in love with, Lotte: but she is already engaged to a man named Albert. Werther stays on from May till September 1771, but then tears himself away and takes up administrative employment with a legation at some unidentified small city (which closely resembles Wetzlar). But he is snubbed by one of the aristocrats there, and hands in his notice. Some months later he returns to the town where Lotte lives. Werther is now totally dominated by his hopeless passion, and, seeing no way out of his predicament, he shoots himself. The events of the novel all take place between May 1771 and December 1772.

As this brief summary makes clear, *Werther* is not overtly concerned with social problems; yet it emphatically bears the imprint of its age. When Werther commits suicide, there is on the table before him a copy of Lessing's *Emilia Galotti* (1772). The first act of that play gives a justly famous portrait of the petty prince as absolute ruler – casually and capriciously dispensing decrees, judgements (even on matters of life and death). Moreover, it is a play that pits against the scandal of princely absolutism the moral seriousness and dignity of bourgeois life. We can assume that Werther aligns himself with the play's perception of class differences, and with its sympathies. He finds himself in a society that offers few outlets for his energies. His one attempt to take employment – significantly in an administrative post attached to a court – ends in humiliation. He is deeply wounded by this experience. He resents the shallowness and snobbery that punishes him for the social solecism of outstaying his welcome in aristocratic company, and above all he is hurt by the offence done to the value and seriousness of his inner life. Not that this rebuff can be made responsible for his tragedy; but the novel does unmistakably see Werther's emotional intensity, his inwardness, his failure to find an appropriate practical channel for his energies as belonging to a particular time and to a particular place. In this novel Goethe offers us not only a timeless drama of the irreconcilability of inner and outer worlds, but also a historical drama in which both worlds are unmistakably identified as belonging to a particular epoch.

Goethe on many occasions lamented the fact that Germany lacked the range and vigour of political and cultural life that would be possible within a unified nation. The ninety-sixth of the bitter epigrammatic poems of satirical import (called *Xenien*) which he and Schiller wrote in the 1790s reads:

> To develop into a nation, that is something you Germans
>   hope for in vain:
> Instead develop yourselves more freely into human beings,
>   that is something you can do.

Werther suggests to us that when someone tries to develop into a full human being – 'ein Mensch' – and finds himself denied the social outlet for his energies, the upshot may be a catastrophic disjunction between self and world. As we shall see, Werther's dilemma was by no means confined to him alone; nor, surprisingly, was it confined to Germany alone.

(b) The culture of inwardness

It is one of the paradoxes of German culture in the second half of the eighteenth century that it is dominated by two seemingly antithetical currents. On the one hand there is the complex of energies known as the Enlightenment ('Aufklärung'), and on the other there is the cult of sensibility known as 'Empfindsamkeit' or Sentimentalism. The enlightenment, which is associated in Germany with the names of Lessing, Nicolai, and Moses Mendelssohn, proclaims a belief in reason, in clear, discursive processes of thought and debate as constituting the avenue to truth: whereas sentimentalism upholds both the dignity and cognitive value of feeling. Despite their manifest differences, however, these two cultural trends have one thing in common: both assert the individual's freedom from established doctrine or received wisdom; both assert that any proposition or tenet or value is true in so far as the individual heart or mind recognizes it as true – no external authority can or should usurp the validating role of individual experience. In a famous programmatic essay of 1784, entitled *What is Enlightenment?*, Kant urges man to 'dare to know', and he sees enlightenment as a process in which man comes of age and becomes truly the arbiter of his own experience. Sentimentalism similarly urges man to have the courage to trust the promptings of his own (feeling) selfhood.

Such a challenge to established authority was felt with particular acuteness in the sphere of religion because it was here that the interplay of public (institutional) demands and private responses was most manifest. From the late seventeenth century on Germany witnesses the growth of one particular form of Protestantism known as Pietism. Pietism placed great stress on the inner life, on self-scrutiny, as the true path to godliness. Many Pietists wrote and published records of their introspection: Francke, Oetinger, Petersen, Spener all produced autobiographies. And thereby they asserted the public interest and worth of private, inward experience. Pietists were particularly active in the field of pedagogics: often their communities founded schools and devoted themselves wholeheartedly to both the theory and the practice of education. Thereby Pietism contributed significantly to the emergence of the culture of sentimentalism in the eighteenth century.

Such a cult of feeling represents a sea-change in the European sensibility, for it asserts that individual psychological processes are worthy in their own right of the most detailed linguistic – and, by extension, literary – expression. Nowadays we take it for granted that literature may legitimately devote itself to the minute portrayal of individuated psychology. But we tend to forget that this kind of concern only emerges gradually in the course of European literature, and that it is bound up with the complex process that is known as secularization. In explaining this process, we have to bear in mind that for many centuries the Christian religion provided the definition and vocabulary for the portrayal of the inner life. With the waning of religion as the chief arbiter of human affairs, secular concerns came into prominence. As a result, inwardness became a psychological rather than a religious matter. Of course, Pietism saw itself as a religious movement; but its effect was to confer dignity on the inner lives not only of mystics and seekers after God, but also of ordinary men and women with their manifestly human promptings. Yet what strikes us today when we read Pietist writings is just how intense and insistent their religious vocabulary is. This is not the vocabulary of modern psychological discourse as we understand it. Rather, the language of Pietism embodies a kind of two-way traffic: religious experience is made secular, but in its turn secular experience is, as it were, theologized. Time and time again the promptings of the heart are endowed with religious significance; and conversely, religious fervour is equated with emotional intensity.

Goethe's *Werther* is one of the supreme expressions of that strange middle ground in which spiritual and secular meet: we are uncertain where one sphere ends and the other begins, the language of one sphere is constantly employed as a metaphor for the other. Of the strength and sincerity of Werther's feelings there can be no doubt; but as to the nature of those feelings, as to the claims that both are and can be made for them, we will find ourselves in uncertain territory. And this is part of the enormous fascination which the novel held for its contemporary readers: for it took issue with the discourse of Pietism and 'Empfindsamkeit'. And still today it obliges us to confront the claims which Werther makes for his experience. Is he simply an overwrought young man? Is he pathologically immature? Does he succumb to the fallacy of confusing strength of feeling with the validity of feeling? Or is it the case that, behind all the self-aggrandizement of his effusive letters, a sombre tragedy of the secularized human spirit is being enacted? Above all, once we enter the extraordinary claustrophobia of his novel, where do we take our stand as we seek to judge Werther, to evaluate the assertions which he unashamedly makes of the dignity and importance of his inner life? Just over two hundred years after its first appearance, *Werther* has lost none of its power to unsettle its readers, to divide them into opposing camps.

Part of the intrusive power of the book derives from the fact that it is written in letter form. We find ourselves buttonholed, cajoled, and harried because Werther seems to be addressing each of us individually. We may despise him or admire him – perhaps, more accurately, we do both. But we cannot remain indifferent.

(c) The novel and its readership

In *Werther* Goethe employs the fiction that an editor figure publishes, with an epilogue, the authentic letters of a young man who committed suicide. In other words, private documents (Werther's letters to his friend Wilhelm) are being made public. This fiction, which is magnificently exploited, was intimately related to the contemporary culture that received the novel so enthusiastically. For it was part of the literary climate of the age that letter-writing was a consuming pastime – just as the pietistic autobiography helped to popularize the notion of people keeping records of their own lives in diary form, in memoirs, recollections, confessions.

The market for literature increased markedly in Germany in the course of the eighteenth century. The book fair in Leipzig is a good barometer – not least because Leipzig was situated in

liberal Saxony. The Leipzig catalogues register the shift in
public taste: from 1740 to 1800 the volume of devotional
literature declined from 19 per cent of total book production to
a mere 6 per cent. In the same period, the total market share of
fictional literature rose sharply. Moreover, the novel came
increasingly into its own. In 1770 38 per cent of all literary
production was devoted to novels: by 1782 the novel's share
had risen to 48 per cent. As the novel moved into the ascendant,
it underwent marked changes in mode and theme. In the first
half of the century adventure novels (so-called 'Robinsonaden'
after their original model, Defoe's *Robinson Crusoe*) were
prominent. But in the second half of the century such novels
began to wane in popularity. The colourful, exotic, and episodic
yarn was replaced by fictional material that invariably claimed
to be authentic. The letter form came to dominate – authenticity, it would seem, was both a property of (claimed)
documentary evidence (that is, the readers were assured by an
editor figure that these were the actual letters written by the
main character), and it was also indissolubly linked with
intimacy of communication: written material felt truthful,
authentic, when it was presented as material written in private.
That such private material was made public did not diminish its
authenticity – because, paradoxically, the public realm was
constituted by the shared acknowledgement of the private
realm as being not only truthful but also valuable. The vogue
for epistolary novels was initiated by Samuel Richardson's
Pamela (1740) and *Clarissa Harlowe* (1747–8) and by
Rousseau's *La nouvelle Héloïse* (1759). Germany was particularly responsive to the appeal of the novel in letters. Knigge,
Miller, Heinse, Jacobi, Gellert, Musäus, Sophie von La Roche
all produced such fictions. By the year 1780 the epistolary novel
dominated, and it was characterized by a mixture of intense
emotion and didacticism. There was a manifest delight in the
immediacy of the letter form. The reader is invited, indeed
obliged, to eavesdrop on the process of writing in which the self
recalls (often in immediate proximity to the events described),
sifts, and evaluates its feelings. At the same time, we are told
that this intimacy with the human heart will prove invaluable

and instructive. The motives, it would seem, that have persuaded the editor to publish these letters are not simply gossipy
or prurient. Rather, 'private' material can serve the function of
'public' edification.

Gradually the novel began to conquer some of the fortresses
of high literary and aesthetic theory, despite the determined
opposition of some of the literary law-givers (such as Gott-
sched). In the same year – 1774 – which saw the publication of
the first edition of *Werther*, there appeared the first major
theoretical tract in German devoted to the theory of the novel
form: Friedrich von Blanckenburg's *Essay on the Novel*. In that
work, Blanckenburg presses the claim for the seriousness of the
novel by insisting that it is capable of exploring the inner life,
the subtle processes of psychological development that occur
within the hero. Blanckenburg esteems Wieland's *Agathon*
(1766–7) as an example of what the novel can achieve: it is not
surprising that *Agathon* should have been grist to Blanckenburg's mill, because it is a novel which scrupulously and
overtly distances itself from the long-winded prose romance
and the 'Robinsonade' (both of which it sees as psychologically
inept and thematically crude). In answer to such outworn
narrative modes Wieland seeks to establish the worth of
psychologically differentiated fiction. In the Preface to his
Secret Journal of 1771 the Swiss pastor and physiognomist
Lavater writes:

a faithful and circumstantial moral [i.e. psychological] history of the
most common and unromantic character is infinitely more important
and fitting for improving the human heart than the most extraordinary
and interesting novel.

Gradually, the novel was evolving into precisely that moral-
cum-psychological history which Lavater was advocating. At
approximately the same time Lessing was seeking to establish
for the drama an aesthetic based on 'Mitleid' or pity. Once
again, it is the reader's (or spectator's) complicity in the inner
processes of the character that makes possible an aesthetic and
human value which no 'mere' sequence of outward events can
achieve.

In a way that contrasted markedly with its English counterpart, German culture continued to resist the novel's struggle for respectability (Schiller, for one, remained largely unconvinced). But in spite of the many rearguard actions, even Germany came, by the end of the eighteenth century, to accept the rehabilitation of the novel. Indeed, in the early years of the nineteenth century a number of writers of the Romantic generation in Germany went so far as to uphold the novel as the supreme literary form of their time. *Werther* was one of the landmarks in its success story.

It is important to establish the context which received *Werther* on its first appearance. The book fell on fertile ground: it addressed a public which was particularly attuned to the interest and excitement of the epistolary novel. Moreover, we have already noted that this climate was by no means unique to Germany: Richardson in England and Rousseau in France had established beyond all doubt the popular appeal and the high seriousness of the novel in letter form. Small wonder, then, that *Werther* proved eminently exportable: the first French translation appeared in 1775, the first English translation in 1779.

Why, in the context of a 'boom' in epistolary novels, should *Werther* have had such an overwhelming impact? Its success was due to the fact that, in a whole variety of ways, it not only capitalized on but took issue with the possibilities inherent in the epistolary novel: *Werther* both reflected and reflected upon its contemporary culture. One of the problems which beset the epistolary novel was that, in order to portray events, conversations, interactions between different people, it had to resort to various (often cumbersome) devices by which a number of correspondents exchanged confidences with each other. *Werther* is distinct in that it takes the radical step of having all the letters written by one and the same person. Goethe's insight is not merely a matter of form: for he focusses the human – that is, moral and psychological – implications of the form with supreme intelligence. Werther's letters are a one-way traffic in the precise sense that this novel is concerned with the defective relationship between the protagonist and the world around him. Goethe appreciates the appalling, claustrophobic fascination of a self for whom letters become the one and only adequate expression. We are persuaded that letters are indeed the appropriate form for Werther's sensibility: there is no action, there are no events or happenings that matter to this particular novel other than those which are presented through the characteristic refractions of his sensibility. Compared with the other epistolary novels of the eighteenth century, *Werther* is electrifying in its brevity and radicalism. And this allows Goethe to exploit the device of the 'editor' to maximum effect. When the editor steps into the story to order and clarify Werther's last frenetic jottings and fragments, when he reports the horror of the mismanaged suicide, we feel ourselves wrenched out of an absorbing, enveloping world into the light of 'real' events and circumstances. The inwardness of 'sentimentalist' culture never received more impassioned advocacy – or more devastating criticism – than in this novel.

Yet we must not simply take the editor figure as the voice of sobriety and detachment. For, in the prefatory note which opens the novel, he commends Werther to us: moreover, in the closing section of the novel, which comes from him, he is not merely the dispassionate onlooker. Despite his role as 'mere' editor, he does also enter the minds of the characters: he obliges us both to stand back from what he reports and at the same time forces us again and again into complicity with the inwardness of the characters. I have already drawn attention to the didacticism of many epistolary novels of the eighteenth century. *Werther*, too, will invite us to learn from the experiences it puts before us, to reflect on what we are told. But the process of judgement is not made easy for us. Rather, we are made to reflect on how we can and do judge; on where we take our stand when we pass judgement; on how we view the power and the sickness of Werther's ravaged sensibility.

These issues are manifold and complex, and I shall return to them later in the sections of detailed analysis. But before we approach the novel itself, there is one final aspect of its relationship to contemporary taste that needs to be discussed. At the end of this study I shall offer a brief discussion of the reception which was accorded *Werther* by its contemporary and subsequent readers. One feature emerges clearly from any discussion of the responses to the work in Goethe's lifetime: time and time again, people asked him about *Werther*, and wanted to know how 'true' it was. We have seen that this notion of 'authentic' material was inseparable from the appeal of the epistolary novel in the eighteenth century. *Werther* draws on this response: but, in one particular way, it was more radical and disturbing than anything its public had ever known before. To enlarge on a point which I have already made in general terms: in the culture of eighteenth-century Germany, the borderlines between public and private material had become blurred. Letters between the poet Klopstock (whose name is invoked at a decisive moment in *Werther*) and his first wife Meta had been published. Goethe in his autobiography *Poetry and Truth* recalls a meeting in 1772 – that is, just before he starts to write *Werther* – at the house of Sophie von La Roche (who one year before had published a hugely popular epistolary novel, *Miss von Sternheim*). At that gathering a man read from his correspondence with his contemporaries. Goethe writes:

He had a number of cases and boxes with him which contained the private correspondence with some friends. There was such a general openness amongst people that one could neither speak nor write to somebody without regarding one's utterance as being directed at several people . . . Such correspondences, particularly with important people, were carefully collected and then, at meetings of friends, were read out in excerpts. And, as political discussions aroused little interest, it was by this means that people came pretty much in contact with letters from the psychological and moral world.

I have already suggested that such a cultural climate nurtured the epistolary novel with its fiction of authenticity. Hence Goethe's *Werther* had as much an immediate purchase on the social world of its readers as does the abundant physical description of streets, houses, rooms in the novels of Balzac or Dickens. But there is more to it than this. Goethe's *Werther* was 'real' in that, as his contemporaries knew full well, it derived from 'real life originals': from Goethe's own love for Charlotte Buff who was engaged to Christian Kestner, from the suicide of a young man called Jerusalem (as we shall see on p. 106 below, the editor's account of the death of Werther is based very closely on Kestner's account, sent as a letter to Goethe, of Jerusalem's last hours). Goethe was, of course, entitled to resent the eager enquiries of readers as to how faithful the novel had been to actual persons and events. But equally, when he did capitalize on his own experience for his novel, he was activating a particular kind of authenticity principle with an uncomfortable truthfulness that accorded with and surpassed the temper of contemporary culture. In this respect, too, *Werther* interlocked with and radicalized its readers' expectations: and, despite the intervening years, despite the fact that we inhabit a very different culture, some of that radicalism can still be felt by us as modern readers.

Chapter 2

The Sorrows of Young Werther

(a) One version or two?

According to Goethe's own account, *Werther* was written in four weeks. It appeared anonymously in Leipzig under the imprint of Weygand (although the catalogue of the Book Fair revealed the authorship) in 1774. Two reprints from the same publisher followed in the same year. In 1775 Weygand produced a 'second genuine edition' whose most important additions were verse mottos which preceded both the first and the second book of the novel. The prefatory poem to the second book is explicit in warning against the seduction of Werther's catastrophic end:

> Du beweinst, du liebst ihn, liebe Seele,
> Rettest sein Gedächtniss von der Schmach;
> Sieh, dir winkt sein Geist aus seiner Höhle:
> *Sei ein Mann, und folge mir nicht nach.*

> (You bemoan him, you love him, dear soul,
> You salvage his memory from disgrace;
> Behold, his spirit signals to you from his cavern:
> *Be a man and do not follow after me.*)

The success of the novel was so great that reprints and pirated editions came thick and fast. Of these the most important was that which appeared from Himburg in Berlin. In 1775 he produced *J. W. Goethe's Works*, without the author's permission, the first part of which contained *Werther*. The text had been slightly modified – certain dialect expressions had, for example, been changed to conform with Berlin usage. In 1777 and 1779 Himburg re-issued the *Works*, and the number of modifications (to say nothing of misprints) increased.

When Goethe began to re-shape the novel in 1782 in Weimar (the second version finally appeared in 1787), he had no copy of the first version to hand. He borrowed from Frau von Stein Himburg's third edition, and had it copied out in order to have a manuscript from which to work. Strangely, then, the basis for Goethe's re-casting of his own novel was an illegal and corrupt text. What is perhaps even stranger is the fact he did not restore many of the linguistic features of the original version. Himburg had, as it were, normalized the German, deleting the abbreviations, elisions, and apostrophes of the 1774 text. And Goethe, it seems, was content with these diminutions of the colloquial force of the original. But he did make a number of important emendations. The prefatory verses (from the second, 1775, Weygand edition) were deleted. The editor figure makes his appearance earlier (after the letter of 6 December in the second version, after that of 17 December in the first). Most of the weighty changes concern the role of the editor and are thus concentrated on the second book of the novel. Where the editor's report in the first version had stressed Albert's coolness towards Lotte, in the second version Albert's character is shown in a more favourable light – and Werther's judgements on him are called into question. This greater distance between the editor and Werther makes itself felt in the report of his decision to commit suicide. The first version reads as follows:

Roughly at this time the decision to leave this world had more completely possessed the soul of the poor young man. It had for a long time been a cherished idea of his, with which he had constantly concerned himself – especially since the return to Lotte.

Yet it was not to be a hasty, swift deed, he wanted to take this step with full conviction, with the greatest possible calmness and certainty.

Whereas the second version reads:

The decision to leave the world had at this time and under such circumstances grown stronger and stronger in Werther's soul. Since the return to Lotte it had always been his last prospect and hope; yet he had said to himself that it should not be a hasty, swift deed, that he wanted to take this step with full conviction, with the greatest possible calmness and certainty.

The changes are small, yet they are significant. The first version is concerned to align us more closely with Werther, whereas the second obliges us to stand back. In the first version we read of

Werther's decision 'to leave this world', which has implications of *this* world and a *next* world, whereas the second version is cooler: 'to leave the world' lacks both the metaphysical implication and the dramatic gesture of narratively encompassing the reader in 'this world of ours'. In the first version, the protagonist is a 'poor young man'; in the second he is simply named. In the first version we read that the decision to take his own life has 'more completely possessed' (the German is 'näher bestimmt') Werther's soul. The phrase is difficult to render effectively in English, implying as it does man in the grip of destiny – a theme dear to Werther's heart. The second version more neutrally says that the decision has 'grown stronger and stronger' ('immer mehr Kraft gewonnen'). The thought of suicide has been 'a cherished idea' ('Lieblingsidee') of Werther's in the first version: in the second it is 'his last prospect and hope' ('seine letzte Aussicht und Hoffnung') – which is tantamount to saying that he has no prospect, no hope. Above all, we should note the contrasting ways in which the two versions report Werther's determination that the deed shall be carefully considered. The first version reads 'yet it *was* not *to be* a hasty, swift deed' ('doch *sollte* es keine übereilte, keine rasche That *seyn*'), and the tense of the verb makes it perfectly possible for us to read this quotation from Werther's thoughts as an utterance that is shared, even validated by the narrator – with the implication of hindsight: 'in the event it turned out to be no hasty, swift deed'. By contrast: the second version insists that we are hearing *only* a quotation from Werther's consciousness, with the addition of 'yet he had said to himself' – and with the subsequent modal verb put in the subjunctive of reported speech: 'doch hatte er sich gesagt, es *solle* keine übereilte, keine rasche Tat *sein*' (yet he had said to himself that it *should* not *be* a hasty, swift deed).

It is also noteworthy that the two versions differ sharply in the way that they report the impact of Werther's failure at court on his already threatened mind. The first version makes much of the offence done to his honour:

He could not forget the frustration that he had experienced at the legation. He mentioned it infrequently, but when he did so even in the most tangential way, one could sense that he felt his honour to have been irretrievably slighted and that this occurrence had given him an aversion to all practical affairs and political activity.

Whereas the second version simply lists this experience as one of a whole number of unfortunate experiences that conspire against Werther: 'Everything unpleasant that had ever befallen him in his active life, the frustration at the legation, everything that had gone awry, that had ever offended him, moved this way and that in his soul.' Where the first version suggests the profound injury done to Werther's capacity for practical activity, the second offers us a mind in thrall to what Kafka calls in the celebrated *Letter to the Father* a 'magnificent congruence of all my bad experiences'.

There is no need to go on cataloguing the differences between the two versions. Clearly, the later version is the work of an older man, and some of the ferocity of the first version is muted. Despite the fact that a number of critics see the first version as more authentic and truthful, I should make clear that in this study I shall concern myself with the second version, and I shall attempt to justify my choice.

Clearly, in the re-writing process Goethe was concerned to modify the balance of sympathies in his readers' response to the text. The interplay of complicity in and detachment from Werther's anguish always was a feature of *Werther* in its various incarnations. It is surely going too far to see the first version as unambiguously siding with Werther and the second version as unambiguously dissenting from him. What Goethe has done in the later version is to make the balance between affirmation and rejection even more delicate than in the first version. To return for a moment to the description of Werther's failure at the legation. The first version, as we have seen, makes more of the slight dealt to Werther's honour. But we should note that even here the German makes clear, by use of the subjunctive mode (which we have noticed in the account given in the second version of Werther's decision to kill himself), that we are hearing Werther's – and not the editor's – reaction: 'so konnte man fühlen, dass er seine Ehre dadurch unwiederbringlich gekränkt hielte' (one could sense that he felt his honour to have been irretrievably slighted). In other words, it is important to see that the first version, too, is capable of maintaining distance between the editor and Werther. In both versions the editor continues with an account of Werther's brooding inactivity and helplessness. Here are the two passages:

So he surrendered entirely to the strange disposition of thought and feeling which we know from his letters, and to an infinite passion before which finally every kind of active energy within him had to evaporate. The eternal sameness of sad meetings with the delightful and beloved creature, whose peace he troubled, the stormy consumption of his forces, with no aim or prospect, impelled him finally to the terrible deed.

. . . and so finally he moved, wholly given over to his strange feeling, thinking, and to an infinite passion, in the eternal sameness of sad meetings with the delightful and beloved creature, whose peace he disturbed, storming at his energies, consuming them with no aim or prospect, so he moved ever closer to a wretched end.

Without attempting a detailed comparison, we note that the first passage consists of two sentences, whereas the second consists of one long sentence unit, sustained by parallel clauses (in fact, English tends to run out of breath, and hence, in my translation, I felt I had to repeat the verb 'so he moved'). In this sense, the second passage feels closer to the rhythms of Werther's own language (which I shall discuss in a later section). But, in fact, the second passage comes from the 1787 version, the first from the 1774 version. My point simply is that we must not succumb to the critical orthodoxy that sees the first version as full-blooded and the second version as detached.

What are we to make of the differing illuminations of Albert's character? Again, I think we should not accept received opinion too quickly. The second version does indeed put Albert in a more favourable light. But this shift in evaluative perspective does more than simply reduce Werther's stature: rather, it deepens the moral dilemma of the whole novel. And it does so by shifting the focus away from the simple 'eternal triangle' model which would suggest that if only Werther had come along earlier, Lotte would not have been engaged to a dry bureaucrat who is temperamentally unsuited to her. Because the second version strengthens Albert's claim on our sympathy, we are made to perceive his unremarkable decency and kindness as a value, which heightens the challenge Werther's sensibility offers to conventional values. Werther's disposition is utterly uncompromising; he calls into question the compromises by which – and within which – most of us (including Albert) live. There is something unconditional about Werther's intensity in both versions. But it is only the second version which makes us see that Albert's limitations are inseparable from his virtues, that the conditions *on* his humanity are also the conditions *of* his humanity. The second version of the novel, much more richly than the first, obliges us to confront these competing claims for our sympathy and assent: Albert's goodness is both more and less of a value than is Werther's unfettered emotional energy.

It is also significant that the second version of the novel gives us much more immediate access to Lotte's inner life than is the case in the first version. In part, as we shall see, this is a question of narrative technique. It is the second version which reveals most powerfully the extent to which Lotte acquiesces in Werther's passion. We are told unequivocally that she has become dependent on him, that she would like to keep him close to her. When, in the scene that immediately precedes Werther's reading of Ossian, she goes through the list of her girl friends to see if she cannot identify a suitable wife for him, she comes to the conclusion that she wants him for herself. The point of such revelations (and, in their explicitness, they have no counterpart in the first version) is not to call Lotte's moral character into question; rather, it is to make us see why Lotte will be terribly deprived when she has to forfeit Werther's company.

Moreover, it should be noticed that, while the editor of the second version is more detached in some of his statements than is his counterpart in the first, the detachment which he expresses is by no means clinical. In the first two pages of his narrative he does indeed, as many critics have pointed out, voice a weighty condemnation of Werther – 'he became a sad companion, ever more unhappy, and ever more unjust the more unhappy he became'. But the editor then immediately qualifies these judgements by writing 'at least, that is what Albert's friends say'. And, a few lines later, when he reports that, despite what Werther claimed, Albert had not changed from the man whom Werther had initially admired and who loved Lotte so profoundly, the editor is at pains to add 'they say' – once again reminding us that we are hearing the judgement of Albert's friends. The editor, then, is concerned less to supply us with ready-made judgements than to confront us with the problem of how we should disentangle and evaluate an intractable emotional tangle. In the second paragraph of his report he tells us that he has collected as much evidence as he could about Werther's last days; he makes clear that the witnesses diverge little in matters of fact and event. But he continues: 'as regards the attitudes of the persons involved, opinions differ and judgements vary'. This, as we shall see later, is true not only of the (fictional) contemporary witnesses but also of subsequent readers.

One final observation about the issue of the two versions of *Werther*. It is only in the second version that we hear the story of the 'Bauernbursch', the young farmhand who loves his mistress, a widow, and who believes that she encourages his love. When he discovers that he has a rival, he kills him. Werther becomes profoundly involved in the case, and when he finds that his pleading is achieving nothing with the judiciary, he identifies with the young man in his despair – 'you are not be saved, wretched man! I see clearly that we are not to be saved.' One objection can immediately be raised to Werther's linking his own destiny with that of the farmhand: the love which this young man feels for the widow is not doomed as is Werther's for Lotte – the object of his love is, after all, potentially available to him, in the sense that there would be no impediment to his marrying her. Perhaps, under this aspect, we should view the 'Bauernbursch' story as a warning to Werther, even as a cautionary tale. That Werther fails to heed the differences between his own situation and that of the farmhand, that he fails to be troubled by the intertwining of passion and fatality, is the measure of his own incapacity for scruple and self-criticism. If we take the 'Bauernbursch' episode this way, then we will see it as part of the greater editorial critique of Werther which is expressed in the second version. But surely the text obliges us also to see this episode as illustrating, and thereby confirming, the sombre tragedy of Werther's passion. His helpless descent into the abyss emerges, then, not simply as an example of individual pathology, but as the expression of a broader human predicament. Many years after writing this novel, Goethe finds himself confronting this tragedy again in one of his supreme poems, the *Trilogy of Passion* (1824). Significantly, he begins the conciliatory poem that closes the sequence by reflecting that, in German, the word 'passion' is linked with the word for 'suffering': 'die Leidenschaft bringt Leiden'. And to that interlocking of passion and suffering, the 'farmhand' episode bears eloquent witness.

Goethe's own response, over the years, to *Werther* in many ways mirrors that of his readers and criticis. Is the novel a moral book, a cautionary tale warning against the dangers of excessive emotion and self-absorption? Or is it ultimately a hymn in praise of untrammelled intensity of being, made in the teeth of all the assumptions, values, and conventions that would seek to condemn it? Perhaps the novel is both – just as the farmhand episode may be seen as both a warning to Werther and a confirmation of him. It almost seems as though, when Goethe included the farmhand's story in the second version, he was thematizing the kinds of response which the 1774 version had elicited from its contemporary public. If he was taking issue with his public's uncertainty as to whether they had been given a moral or an immoral book, he did so without resolving the issue one way or the other. For the tale of the farmhand belongs unmistakably to the unnerving balance of the 1787 version. Goethe surely had something of this in mind when, in a letter of May 1783 to Kestner, he spoke of the re-writing process:

I have in peaceful hours taken out my *Werther*, and I think that, without tampering with any of the things that caused so much of a sensation, I can, by a number of turns, lift it to a still higher plane ['ihn noch einige Stufen höher . . . schrauben']. Amongst other things it was my intention in the process to portray Albert in such a way that the impassioned youth may misunderstand him – but the reader will not. This will have the desired – and the best – effect. I hope you will be pleased.

The modifications, as we have seen, entail not a simple change of the affirmation of Werther into a critique of him, but rather an enrichment of the complex interplay of human sympathies in the novel. Albert becomes a more agreeable character, which serves to highlight Werther's egocentricity; but Lotte is shown to be more implicated in Werther's passion, which suggests the human worth of such an unconditional feeling. The editor is more of a detached onlooker, yet he also moves closer to the inner world of the human psyche. The upshot is an amazing act of artistic balance and moral differentiation. In the pages that follow I hope to explore the many ways in which the scrupulously controlled balance of sympathies in *Werther* makes it one of the most remarkable novels of world literature.

(b) Werther the writer

With the exception of the pages of editorial narrative and commentary which form the concluding section of the novel, everything that we know of Werther we gather from his own account of his experiences as mediated through his letters to Wilhelm. Indeed, the writing of letters is the activity on which he expends the greater part of his energies. Above all else, Werther is a self who writes, who discovers and in part defines himself through writing. Much of the drama of the novel is transmitted through the fluctuations of mood and style which chart the ebb and flow of Werther's sense of himself. It is one of the most painful aspects of the book that psychological disintegration becomes palpable in the disintegration of Werther's discourse. The letter of 10 May in the first book shows him at his most expansive:

Eine wunderbare Heiterkeit hat meine ganze Seele eingenommen, gleich den süssen Frühlingsmorgen, die ich mit ganzem Herzen geniesse. Ich bin allein und freue mich meines Lebens in dieser Gegend, die für solche Seelen geschaffen ist wie die meine. Ich bin so glücklich, mein Bester, so ganz in dem Gefühle von ruhigem Dasein versunken, dass meine Kunst darunter leidet. Ich könnte jetzt nicht zeichnen, nicht einen Strich, und bin nie ein grösserer Maler gewesen als in diesen Augenblicken. Wenn das liebe Tal um mich dampft und die hohe Sonne an der Oberfläche der undurchdringlichen Finsternis meines

Waldes ruht und nur einzelne Strahlen sich in das innere Heiligtum stehlen, ich dann im hohen Grase am fallenden Bache liege und näher an der Erde tausend mannigfaltige Gräschen mir merkwürdig werden; wenn ich das Wimmeln der kleinen Welt zwischen Halmen, die unzähligen unergründlichen Gestalten der Würmchen, der Mückchen näher an meinem Herzen fühle und fühle die Gegenwart des Allmächtigen, der uns nach seinem Bilde schuf, das Wehen des Alliebenden, der uns in ewiger Wonne schwebend trägt und erhält; mein Freund, wenn's dann um meine Augen dämmert und die Welt um mich her und der Himmel ganz in meiner Seele ruhn wie die Gestalt einer Geliebten, dann sehne ich mich oft und denke: Ach, könntest du das wieder ausdrücken, könntest du dem Papier das einhauchen, was so voll, so warm in dir lebt, dass es würde der Spiegel deiner Seele, wie deine Seele ist der Spiegel des unendlichen Gottes! – Mein Freund! – Aber ich gehe darüber zugrunde, ich erliege unter der Gewalt der Herrlichkeit dieser Erscheinungen.

(A wondrous serenity has taken possession of all my soul, like the sweet spring mornings which I enjoy with all my heart. I am alone and I rejoice in my life in this region which is meant for such souls as mine. I am so happy, oh best of friends, so immersed in a feeling of tranquil existence that my art suffers because of it. I could not draw now – not a single line, and I have never been a greater painter than in these moments. When the lovely valley breathes its mists around me and the high sun rests on the impenetrable darkness of my forest and only solitary rays of light steal into the inner sanctuary, and I then lie in the tall grass by the tumbling river and, being closer to the earth, I find that thousand manifold grasses catch my eye; when I feel closer to my heart the teeming movements of the miniature world between the stalks and grasses, the countless unfathomable shapes of the grubs, of the midges, and feel the presence of the Almighty who made us in his image, feel the moving breath of the All-loving One who holds us and keeps us hovering in eternal bliss; my friend, when it then darkens about my eyes and the world around me and the sky rest utterly in my soul like the figure of a beloved – then I am frequently filled with longing and think: Ah, if you could only re-create that, if you could breathe on to the paper that which lives so abundantly, so warm within you that it might be the mirror of your soul, just as your soul is the mirror of the infinite God! – My friend – But I am broken by all this, I succumb to the might of the splendour of these phenomena.)

The primary experience of this letter is Werther's discovery, in closeness to nature, of the sheer abundance of the created world. The mood is exultant and the letter celebrates a merging of the self into the natural world.

The opening sentence establishes the two key notions which

dominate the whole letter: plenitude and kinship. A human emotion ('Heiterkeit') is likened to natural phenomena ('*gleich* den süssen Frühlingsmorgen'), and twice the adjective of totality – 'ganz' – is heard ('meine ganze Seele', 'mit ganzem Herzen'). In human terms, the speaker is solitary ('allein'), but that solitude is offset by communion with the natural landscape which is, so he tells us, made for such souls as his. The relationship between man and nature is a major theme of the novel: one characteristic strand of that theme is evident here – the notion that nature is the corroboration and extension of the human heart. The third and fourth sentences register a price to be paid in and for that merging of self and world: Werther's art suffers. His absorption in the world around him prevents him from picturing that world in paint on paper. The loss of contours between self and world means that phenomena lose their defining edges: there are no lines any more, no demarcations between one entity and another. Yet, paradoxically, Werther asserts that he has never been a greater artist than in such moments. The paradox derives from the equation of art with its inward preconditions, with the state of mind and heart of the artist – which is to ignore the correlative of that spirit in outward activity, in creative making. Werther's condition of ecstatic closeness to nature does, it seems, withdraw him from specifically human society (he is alone) and from specifically human activity (painting, picturing the world).

Yet the letter makes clear that one form of picturing the world is still available to Werther – language. The statement of his lack of artistic creativity is immediately followed by an enormous sentence of parallel clauses ('when . . .', 'when . . .') which name and enact the fullness of the world. The 'wenn' clauses list natural phenomena as related and revealed to the self, and the main clause – 'dann sehne ich mich oft' (then I am frequently filled with longing) – chronicles the response of the human subject to nature. The sentence captures an ecstatic surrender to the scale of the world, and at the same time contains that ecstasy within the firm grammatical housing of German word order and syntax. This is the kind of sentence structure that is associated with Pietism (and particularly with sermons in the grandiose homiletic mode), with Klopstock's poetry and, of course, with Werther. It is particularly difficult to translate – principally because, in English, the parallel clauses lack the underpinning through word order which signals their place in a large and complex sentence.

The 'wenn' clauses all instance the reciprocity between the self and nature: the first 'wenn' unit makes natural phenomena the subject of four of the clauses (the valley, the sun, the rays, the grasses), but one clause has the 'ich' as subject ('ich dann . . . liege'). But even where nature is the grammatical subject, the 'ich' is omnipresent – 'around *me*', '*my* forest', 'catch *my* eye'. In the second 'wenn' unit (separated from the first clause sequence by a semi-colon), the 'ich' is the subject of the clauses, is the active (i.e. perceiving) agent: the grammatical objects are minute natural phenomena (grubs, insects). But the registering of this microscopic world leads on to a perception of the cosmic architect of all this life. The pulse of the sentence quickens as this crucial transition is made though the repetition of the verb 'fühlen': 'wenn ich das Wimmeln . . . die . . . Gestalten . . . fühle, und fühle die Gegenwart des Allmächtigen'. Strictly speaking, the syntactical rules of the German subordinate clause would demand that the verb should be placed at the end of the clause – 'und die Gegenwart des Allmächtigen *fühle*'. The slight disturbance of grammatical rules signals a change in feeling. The organ of perception which registers the insects and the presence of God may be one and the same – it is the heart, which 'feels and feels' – but the syntactic shift marks the move from one order of being and experience to another.

Once again a semi-colon signals the end of a unit of clauses. And it is followed immediately by an exclamation 'mein Freund!' – which would seem to indicate that the enormous sentence is poised to turn about its grammatical axis and to embark on the main clause. But we are deceived: for there is one further unit of 'wenn' clauses to come. And these clauses are like a murmured incantation which enshrine the blissful loss of self in a greater union: 'wenn's dann um meine Augen dämmert' (when it then darkens about my eyes). 'Dämmern' will recur throughout the novel, and it will signal a state in which separateness gives place to union, in which borderlines are obliterated. The world, Werther tells us, and the sky ('Himmel' in German means sky and heaven: the English translator does not have such a compound meaning at his disposal), rest within him like a beloved (the German 'der Geliebten' signals the gender as feminine). Again we hear the intimation of totality – 'ganz' – which was present in the opening sentence of the letter. We note the movement of the prepositions as what surrounded the self '*um* meine Augen', '*um* mich her' comes to rest '*in* meiner Seele'. Now the great sequence of 'wenn' clauses is complete: a dash marks off the main clause – 'dann sehne ich mich oft'. Yet, strangely, the main clause, occurring as it does immediately after the last 'wenn' unit which celebrates rapt, almost erotic union, does not heighten the mood of achieved oneness, nor does it even continue it. Rather it announces a need which, because of its grammatical mode and prefatory exclamation – 'Ach, könntest du . . .' – is clearly signalled as unattainable: the need to express on paper (perhaps with paint, as in the third and fourth sentence, or in words) the warm and abundant inner life of the heart. Again the subjunctive is heard ('dass es würde') and expresses the unreal wish that the reciprocity between the soul and God could be captured on paper, so that the paper could mirror the human and divine mirroring. The note of regret dominates the closing sentence of the letter, with its notion of the self being broken as it succumbs to a splendour that is excessive and even threatening ('Gewalt' implies tyrannical force). The 'Erscheinungen' (the German word can mean both 'phenomena' and 'manifestations') threaten to overwhelm the self.

This letter, occurring as it does in one of the first great works of modern German literature, is a remarkable, and precocious, tribute to the expressive range of the German language (and, as I have tried to make clear, it is a range that frequently leaves English gasping for breath). It captures an ecstasy of spirit that almost (but not quite) bursts the bounds of German syntax. One feels the pressure of experience straining against the confines of language, yet the intensity of feeling and vision is triumphantly contained and sustained. The contrast with some of the later letters is nothing short of heartbreaking: the language becomes dislocated and fragmentary, and mirrors all too painfully the disarray in the self. Admittedly, the warning signs are present even in this jubilant early letter: the ominous implication that a merging of self and world can lead to a loss of both self and world is not far to seek. And Werther's lament for his failure to find adequate expression for his perceptions vibrates with larger implications: what is at stake here is not only his ability or inability as a creative artist, but an imbalance between the experiencing and reflective self. As I hope to show later, Werther is not only a man of spontaneous and sincere feeling: he is also someone who is unremittingly self-conscious: he knows that he feels; and he knows that he knows.

Yet we must be on our guard against bringing too much hindsight to bear: we must not reduce the ecstatic early letters to mere prefigurative symptoms of his catastrophic end. Clearly a letter such as that of 10 May constitutes a major linguistic (and human) achievement. It is part of the emotional and artistic balance of the novel that we are asked to assent to Werther's intensity of feeling and perception as constituting a value (not the only one in human affairs, nor one that provides orientation for daily living, but a value nonetheless). And we need to have this value in mind when we come to a later letter which provides an explicit echo of the one we have just considered in detail, the letter of 18 August in the first book. This letter repeats the syntactical signature of the 10 May letter in that it, too, operates with an extended parallelism of 'wenn' clauses. Moreover, the links are more than simply syntactical. We are reminded of the perceptions of the May letter; the thematic echoes are unmistakable in the references to the 'millions of swarming midges', to the 'splendid forms of the infinite world', 'the unfathomable forces', 'the races of manifold creatures'. Yet the mood of the 18 August letter is elegiac: it feels valedictory because the verbs are, for the greater part, in the past tense, and the force of the past is pointed up by the contrast between 'now' ('jetzt') and 'then' ('ach damals'). The present perception expressed in the August letter is one of nature as 'an eternally devouring, eternally chewing, ruminating monster'. What the two letters have in common is the fact that they both comprehend nature as corroborating and magnifying human moods. But the gulf between 10 May and 18 August is terrifying. We only register its enormity if we recall the earlier letter and all it expressed as something intrinsically valuable. Because only then do we appreciate Werther's decline both as a psychological process particular to one man, and also as a larger tragedy of the human spirit. And central to the latter must be our perception that Werther's is a 'noble mind' which 'is here o'erthrown.'

(c) *Werther* as a psychological study

I have just suggested that *Werther* must be seen as, at one level, a character study of one particular individual, and, at another level, as a larger, tragic analysis of the human predicament. I want now to concentrate on the first aspect. If we view Werther in psychological terms, we will find ourselves obliged to be critical of his character and temperament, and to register the sickness of spirit which removes him further and further from any genuine contact with the world (both human and natural) around him. The story *Werther* tells, with extraordinary ferocity, is one of increasing isolation, of a solipsism which, paradoxically but necessarily, loses all hold even on the one entity it cherishes above all else: the self. And, in a last desperate act of assertion, the self becomes the agent of its own obliteration.

Time and time again Werther inveighs against the constricted condition ('Einschränkung' is the key term) in which men are forced to spend their lives. The theme first sounds in the letter of 22 May (in the first book). There, in the opening paragraph, Werther refers to the 'constriction in which the active and inquiring energies of man are imprisoned'. The letter closes on a sombre note: 'however constricted [man] may be, he still always retains in his heart the sweet feeling of freedom, that he can leave this prison when he wishes to'. It is one of the supreme ironies of the novel that Werther, in his reaction against the conditions which conspire to fetter his spirit, imprisons himself the more terribly in an ever-narrowing world of his own making. The thought of suicide is present in Werther's mind from early on – indeed, as this letter demonstrates, it is there even before Werther meets Lotte. And this surely makes it clear that Werther's suicide is not simply the result of an unhappy love affair with a girl whom he cannot possess. The doomed love is part of – and symptomatic of – a more profound dislocation between Werther and the life around him.

Time and time again, as Werther seeks to combat the constriction of mundane circumstances, he is forced to supplant the outside world, which is resistant to his wishes, by a surrogate world that is made in his own image. His longing for absorption into and oneness with the world around him degenerates into a refusal to recognize the otherness of people, places, and situations. In the process, he loses all hold on phenomenal reality: Werther is so concerned to know life through essential, unconditional experience that he scorns the distance that separates, and by separating, defines, the contours of the self and the other. The quest for strenuously authentic experience leads him to live in an invented world. All this becomes manifest in the last letters: as Werther plans his suicide, so he allots to those around him their appropriate roles: he claims to be dying for Lotte, he asks that the children be told the 'fate of their unhappy friend', he urges nature to mourn her 'son, friend, and lover', he associates his death with Christ's passion. This is the culmination of the sick fantasy that only allows the world to exist in a scenario written for it by the self. Goethe's imaginative understanding of this kind of sickness – and of how this sickness grows from much that is fine and valuable in Werther's temperament – is nothing short of astonishing.

The events portrayed in the novel cover something over a year. Within this brief temporal compass Goethe contrives to chart the often feverish graph of Werther's decline. Certain key thematic clusters serve to plot the various stages in the process. And I want now to trace these themes.

I shall begin with nature, not least because it was necessarily at the forefront of our discussion of the 10 May letter. It will be remembered that, in that letter, Werther speaks of his rapturous discovery of the abundance in nature which implicitly expresses an immanent deity. This register predominates in the early letters. But gradually the discordant note which we observed in the 10 May letter becomes stronger. In the letter of 24 July (in the first book) Werther speaks almost incredulously of his closeness to nature as entailing a loss of precise perception of discrete phenomena:

> Never was I happier, never was my feeling in response to nature – right down to the smallest stone or grass – fuller or more intense, and yet – I do not know how to put it – my ability to hold fast to images is so weak, everything floats and wavers so before my soul that I cannot hold on to any outline.

In this passage the formulation of Werther's impassioned response to nature is revealing: it is an 'Empfindung an der Natur' – a 'feeling in response to nature' – but it is not a sense *of* nature. The prepositional construction 'an der' is suggestive, for it implies that the feeling is at one remove from nature, the occasion of that feeling. The sense of a disturbed relationship between the self and the natural world grows stronger as the novel progresses, although, as his mood darkens towards the end, Werther still continues to seek confirmation of his inner state in nature. I have already referred to the letter of 18 August (in Book One) which, in effect, takes back the 10 May letter, and replaces the perception of nature as teeming life with that of nature as ineluctable law of death and decay. In Book Two, the letter of 21 August, Werther again speaks of oneness with nature – and he does so with those characteristic phrases ('in mir', 'um mich her') that we noted in the 10 May letter: 'Ja, es ist so. Wie die Natur sich zum Herbste neigt, wird es Herbst in mir und um mich her. Meine Blätter werden gelb.' (Yes, it is so. As nature declines towards autumn, so it becomes autumn within me and around me. My leaves are turning yellow.) The confirmatory relationship between the self and nature is still upheld; but the bond provides no solace, no relief: nature is simply Werther's decline writ large. He does not perceive that nature is both an eternally devouring monster and a source and symbol of abundant life. In one terrifying moment Werther realizes that nature, as he perceives it, is not an objective entity at all, but simply an inert picture: 'when this splendid nature stands so rigid before me like a little lacquered picture and all the bliss cannot pump a single drop of happiness into my brain . . .' (letter of 3 November, Book Two). The Werther of the final letters reverts to the dark 'pathetic fallacy' of the letter of 18 August: he envisages nature as caught up in the elegiac lament for his death. But by the time we reach these final letters we have been made to understand the appalling truth that Werther so steadfastly conceals from himself: that his frequently asserted intimacy with nature is ultimately little better than a fascination with images of the natural world that are of his own making. And this takes us back to that ecstatic outpouring of 10 May in which Werther greets a region 'which is meant for such souls as mine'. Where that letter held out the promise of a rich discovery of the manifold orders of being within nature, the later letters suggest that Werther is simply plundering the outer world for confirmation of the promptings of his own selfhood.

The second important thematic cluster concerns Werther and love. In the famous scene (one which was to prove particularly attractive to the illustrators of the novel) where Werther sees Lotte for the first time, she is in a domestic role: surrounded by children, she is distributing slices of bread and butter. This domesticity accounts in large measure for Lotte's hold on Werther's mind and imagination: he loves her for precisely the things that are denied him, for her secure anchorage in the simple, practical world of hearth and home. And this gives point to the remarks which Lotte makes to Werther in the long scene, reported by the editor, which occurs immediately after the letter of 20 December (in Book Two). She says: 'Be a man, turn this sad dependence away from a creature who can do nothing but pity you'; and again: 'Why me, Werther? Why me in particular, the property of somebody else? Why particularly this? I fear, I fear that it is only the impossibility of possessing me which makes the wish so attractive to you.' The implications of the seeming paradox which Lotte here expresses – that

Werther loves her because she is unattainable – are both arresting and important. The thought of Werther settling into orderly domesticity with Lotte is somewhat unreal. Perhaps she has come to sense that he loves her for being the symbol of a realm of human experience which he reveres but which he can no more enter than he can contemplate any compromise with all the various other demands of limited, practical activity. In this sense we could say that Werther loves Lotte as an image, as some projected ideal of wish-fulfilment: certainly the novel makes us doubt if Werther could ever begin to cope with the demands of living with the sheer otherness of a real person. The solipsism which we have noted in Werther's relationship to nature is, then, also present in his love for Lotte. In the letter of 13 July, Book One, Werther persuades himself that Lotte loves him, that her 'sympathy for [him] and [his] fate' amounts to love. And he adds the revealing comment: 'how valuable I become in my own eyes, how I – I can say it to you, you can understand such things – how I worship myself since she loves me.' What is invoked here is the reciprocity of love, the mutual enhancement of the selves of the two lovers. But it is difficult for us to banish from our mind the possibility that Werther may be succumbing to a delusion, to self-aggrandizement ('how I worship myself'). In the second book of the novel there is a particularly revealing letter (3 September) which consists of but one sentence: 'I sometimes do not understand how someone else *can* – *may* – love her, given that I alone love her, so fully, so intensely, and know nothing else, understand nothing else, have nothing else but her!' Here Werther expresses his sheer incomprehension that the self is not the legislator for other people's behaviour: he is bemused that there is somebody *other* ('ein anderer') who has claims to make on Lotte, because, for Werther, there is nothing other than his feeling and knowing – 'nichts anders kenne, noch weiss, noch habe als sie'. Twice in the compass of one sentence, the notion of otherness is invoked: and each time the other is swamped in a veritable barrage of negatives ('ich begreife . . *nicht*, *nichts* anders kenne, *noch* weiss, *noch* habe'). As the ending of the novel makes clear, Werther takes his own life in a desperate assertion of the self in repudiation of all resistant otherness: what he does not realize is that to forfeit the other is also to forfeit the self.

The theme of Werther and love takes us into territory similar to that charted by the theme of Werther and nature. Both themes oblige us to perceive Werther critically. And yet, just as in respect of nature we found that Werther's increasing self-centredness was the cankered version of what began as a genuine and revelatory closeness to nature, so too any consideration of Werther and love obliges us to recognize a value behind all the distortions of a threatened sensibility. And this becomes crucially important in any assessment of the role that Lotte plays in the novel. What prevents her from being the simple paragon of domesticity, what prevents her from being merely a mirage of Werther's fevered imaginings (both domestic and erotic) is precisely the fact that she does become emotionally involved with him against so many of the dictates of her better judgement. The editor's prelude to the scene in which Werther reads aloud from his translation of Ossian goes a long way towards clarifying the character and extent of her emotional entanglement, and the dilemma which it enshrines.

The editor begins with her feelings about Albert: 'She saw herself now eternally joined to the man whose love and loyalty she knew, to whom she was devoted with all her heart, whose calmness, whose reliability seemed to be fully ordained by Heaven for a decent woman to base the happiness of her life upon; she felt what he would always be to her and her children.' It is important to note the key terms in this passage – 'loyalty', 'calmness', 'reliability'. These words are – and in context they are unambiguously intended to be – terms of approbation. Albert is, indeed, a good husband: he is the kind of man to whom Lotte rightly clings because part of her needs the anchorage in the domestic sphere within which Albert makes supreme sense as her marital partner. I have already commented on the ways in which the figure of Albert becomes more positive in the changes made from the first to the second version of the novel. He does, indeed, stand for admirable qualities: and the editor insists, in his account of Lotte's thoughts, that we see those qualities not as the components of a sterile conformism, but for what they are: values which sustain and support lives housed within the modest dimensions of practical living. But the editor also knows – and he demands that we share in that knowledge – that there are other kinds of value. Those are put before us when we are acquainted with Lotte's thoughts about Werther:

On the other hand Werther had become so precious to her, from the very first moment of their acquaintance, the consonance of their temperaments had shown itself so beautifully, the long lasting contact with him, the many situations they had lived through together – all this had left its indelible imprint on her heart. Everything interesting that she felt or thought she was wont to share with him, and the prospect of his leaving threatened to tear a hole in her whole being which could not be filled. Oh, if only she had been able at that moment to change him into her brother! If only she could have married him to one of her friends, she could have hoped to restore his relationship with Albert!

We note, in the very first sentence, the quickening of emotion in the little intensifying particle '*so* precious', '*so* beautifully'. On a first reading, we might expect a consecutive clause – 'so precious that . . .' But there is no following 'that' clause. The 'so' celebrates intensity of experience, pure and simple. We note also the strength of the language: the imprint on Lotte's heart is 'indelible', to be deprived of him would be to 'tear a hole in her whole being'. As Lotte tries to take stock of her feelings for Werther, she is unable to offer a cool, sober assessment. The passion of her attachment to him generates passionate thoughts. And the emotion rises to a climax in the last two sentences of our quotation. Suddenly we forget the presence of the editor as mediating figure, for we hear Lotte's own thoughts as they take shape in her brain – in the mode of 'if only she could . . .' We are here confronted by the narrative device that is called free indirect speech ('style indirect libre', or 'erlebte Rede').

Free indirect speech combines the utterance or thought of a character with the discourse of a third person narrator (in this case the editor figure). Perhaps, for purposes of simple illustration, I may be allowed to invent an example. Let us assume that the following passage is the opening of a novel:

Charles was walking down Oxford Street in the gentle September sunshine. Suddenly he stopped in his tracks. Was that not the man he had seen yesterday talking to the pigeons in Trafalgar Square? Charles shook his head and walked on.

The first, second, and fourth sentences are couched in the mode of traditional third-person narrative. And this mode conditions our perspective on the character: we stand outside and observe him – he is, as it were, 'over there'. Now, of course, most third-person narrators are not content to be mere onlookers. Often they choose to take us inside the mind of a character. They can do this by a straightforward act of reporting in indirect speech. We could re-write our third sentence as follows: 'He asked himself if that was not the man he had seen the day before . . .' Or, alternatively, the narrator could report Charles's thoughts in direct speech: 'He thought: "Isn't that the man I saw yesterday . . ."' But there is a third possibility for conveying the perceptions of a fictional character: and it is the one which is employed in my quotation. What the narrator has done is to adopt Charles's own form of words – 'isn't that the man I saw yesterday' – but to retain the past tense, and the third person of his narrative account ('*was* that not the man *he had* seen'). But he leaves everything else in Charles's original formulation ('yesterday' and not 'the day before'). Moreover, the narrator has refrained from signalling clearly that he is quoting Charles's perceptions and not his own (there is no 'he thought', 'he wondered'). In other words, although there is no obvious break between the second and third sentences, we, the readers, instantly recognize that the narrator is allowing us a glimpse into the inner life of the character. This third possibility is known as free indirect speech.

Let us return now to the last two sentences of the editor's report of Lotte's attitude to Werther. Clearly what she thinks is: 'könnte ich ihn zum Bruder umwandeln' (if only I could change him into my brother). And the editor makes us hear the full force of Lotte's fervent wish by quoting what we recognize to be her own words. The tenses and the pronouns remain those of the editor; but even so, we know that, for the duration of those two sentences of desperate (and unreal) wishing, we are drawn into Lotte's mind. It is almost as though the force of her passion invades the discourse of editorial control and distance. We hear Lotte's voice more than we do the editor's.

A few pages later the same device recurs, and again it is employed to acquaint us with Lotte's inner turmoil. After the scene of the Ossian reading she finds it impossible to regain her emotional equilibrium. She sleeps very badly, and the following day sees her no calmer:

Her blood which normally flowed so purely and sweetly was in feverish uproar, a thousand different feelings churned in her lovely heart. Was it the ardour of Werther's embraces that she felt in her breast? Was it irritation with his boldness? Was it a regretful comparison of her present condition with those days of completely easy, unclouded innocence and serene trust in herself? How should she meet her husband, how should she confess to him a scene which she could so easily admit to – and yet which she did not trust herself to admit to?

The editor continues in this vein for several sentences before abandoning free indirect speech and resuming his usual narrative mode. And he goes on to tell us that, because of scruple and self-doubt on Lotte's part, because of Albert's evidently irritable mood, there is no open, frank communication between husband and wife that evening. A degree of diffidence – perhaps even of estrangement – comes between them. Then Werther's note arrives, requesting the loan of Albert's pistols. This immediately compounds Lotte's anguish – and her silence. Nothing has been said, nothing can be said, and the pistols are sent. As the editor grimly reflects, had husband and wife only been able to talk, 'perhaps our friend could still have been saved'.

This is a quite magnificent scene, one that, in a very brief compass, sketches a small tragedy within bourgeois marriage. The equivalent scene in the first version of *Werther* does not come anywhere near the power and complexity of what the second version offers. In the first version, the silence between husband and wife is simply caused by Lotte's embarrassment and Albert's coldness:

Against her will she felt deep in her heart the ardour of Werther's embraces, and immediately the days of her unclouded innocence, of serene trust in herself appeared before her eyes with redoubled loveliness, and, in advance, she was afraid of the glances of her husband, of his half irritated, half mocking questions when he would learn about Werther's visit.

Moreover, there are no passages of free indirect speech in the first version which would bring us right inside Lotte's consciousness (and conscience). The second version gains immeasurably from the employment of free indirect speech. That gain is a matter not just of technical (narrative) variety, not just of greater psychological insight into Lotte. The implications are profounder than this, and they have to do with the fact that the passages of free indirect speech affect us very powerfully as readers. For, at such moments, the editor's voice is, as it were, overridden by Lotte's; and, in consequence, we have the sense of a mould being shattered, of passion making inroads into established language and consciousness. This is the linguistic and narrative correlative of precisely that effect which Werther has had on Lotte. He has invaded her very being. She may resent the inroads, she may resist them: but they are there, and the wound is real. The penultimate sentence of the novel reads: 'there were fears for Lotte's life'. The passages in free indirect speech tell us that those fears are justified.

Once we perceive the extent of Lotte's involvement with Werther, we see her as a flesh-and-blood character and not simply as a cipher for imperturbable innocence. In the letter of 30 July of the first book, Werther reflects that Lotte had, in all likelihood, been putting in a good word for him with Albert: 'women are clever at that, and they are right, if they can ensure that two admirers get on well with each other, then it is to their advantage – however rarely it comes about'. What may seem to be simply an uncharacteristic utterance of wordly cynicism on Werther's part acquires greater point when we see that it has a measure of justification: Lotte does, indeed, want to keep both admirers. There is also the incident reported in the letter of 12 September (Book Two), when Lotte shows Werther how her canary takes its seed from her – and from Werther's – lips. The transferred kiss is hardly innocent – as she has reason to know full well. We surely cannot help agreeing with Werther when he comments 'she should not do it'. We must also think of the moment when, immediately after the passage of free indirect speech which we have just discussed, the editor tells us that Lotte goes through the list of her friends in quest of a suitable wife for Werther. He then makes explicit what the reader has presumably suspected: 'in all these musings she came to feel – without making it clear to herself – that her heartfelt and secret desire was to keep him for herself, and she also said to herself that she could not, should not keep him'.

Such moments do not suggest that Lotte is flighty or flirtatious, nor do they serve to stifle our critical perceptions of Werther and his relationship to Lotte. But they do spell out for us the very real dilemma which Lotte faces. That dilemma is acute because, despite all his posturings and self-indulgence, Werther insists on the value and beauty of unconditional experience; and for somebody such as Lotte, who does admit such claims, to be deprived of Werther is to forfeit a whole dimension of experience. If intensity can be a value in and of itself, then there is a sense in which Werther is, as his name implies, 'worthy'.

To trace the theme of Werther and love through the novel, then, is to find oneself confronting a number of complex and difficult questions. At one level, we perceive the blight of Werther's increasing solipsism, his inveterate habit of self-projection which means that he loves not a real person but his image of that person. But on another level, when we observe Lotte's reactions, we must recognize that, in his uncompromising (and, indeed, selfish) demands, Werther does capture whole areas of her heart and mind. That Lotte is persuaded to cherish Werther not in spite of but because of his wilfulness is a challenge to our criticism of Werther.

One of the bonds that unite Werther and Lotte is their shared delight in literature – above all in literature of a particular kind. And this brings me to the next theme I wish to consider: Werther and art. At one point Lotte speaks both for herself and for Werther when she says: 'that author is dearest to me in whom I re-discover my world, in whose works things occur as they do around me' (16 June, Book One). Here Lotte speaks of the kind of literature that both confirms and illuminates her experience. The context makes clear that she is thinking primarily of literature that cherishes the domestic sphere which she inhabits (Goldsmith's *The Vicar of Wakefield* is mentioned as an example). In the early part of the novel Werther too shares the love for a literature that upholds a simple, primal world, one whose idyllic strain serves to confirm the rightness of man's being in the world of modest events and circumstances. In the letters of 13 May, 26 May, 21 June Werther praises Homer for his affirmation of anchored, patriarchal existence. But we note that gradually Homer is replaced in Werther's affections by Ossian. In the letter of 12 October (Book Two) we read: 'Ossian has supplanted Homer in my heart. What a world into which this splendid man leads me!' For Werther, the relationship to literature is (as his relationship to so much else) all or nothing. He seems incapable of cherishing both Homer and Ossian: the one excludes the other. It is the measure of the gulf that yawns between Werther and the world around him that he assents totally to Ossian's elegiac lament for a blighted world. In a conversation with Henry Crabb Robinson of 1829 Goethe commented to his English visitor: 'it was never perceived by the critics that Werther praised Homer while he retained his senses, and Ossian when he was going mad'. At one level, the point is a valid one: the change in Werther's reading habits bespeaks a change in his emotional well-being.

However, the Goethe who spoke somewhat testily to Crabb Robinson was only expressing one facet of the Ossian phenomenon: what *Werther* captures – with extraordinary force – is the extent to which, as part of the phenomenon of secularization which I have already discussed in my opening chapter, secular literature was invested with a well-nigh canonical authority. This process is by no means confined to Werther alone. There are two decisive moments in his relationship to Lotte when literature in the form of the 'cult book' brings them closer together. In the letter of 16 June from the first book, Werther reports the moment when both he and Lotte stand by the windows and look out on a landscape refreshed by a recent thunderstorm:

she looked towards heaven and then at me, I saw her eyes fill with tears, she laid her hand on mine and said: 'Klopstock'. I immediately recalled the splendid ode which was in her thoughts, and I sank into a torrent of feeling which she had poured out over me with this password. I could bear it no longer, I bent over her hand and kissed it, shedding the most blissful tears. And I looked into her eyes again – Oh noble man! Had you but seen the worship in her glance, and would that I should never again hear your name which has been so often sullied.

The language here is quite explicitly that of religious veneration. Klopstock, through his famous ode *Die Frühlingsfeier* (*The Celebration of Spring*) is the catalyst that both liberates and confirms the emotion of these two young people. They are believers, united in their faith, in their shared response to Klopstock's poetry. However much Lotte, in the remark which I quoted earlier, values literature which confirms the simple domestic round of her life, she is also attuned to the great visionary promise of Klopstock's poetry, to its grandiose intimations of the immanence of God in nature. And, as a later passage makes clear, she is also susceptible to the voice of the human spirit grieving for the desolation all around it. I have in mind the second emotional high point brought about by literature, when Werther, at Lotte's bidding, reads out loud from his own translation of Ossian (which he has given into Lotte's safekeeping). This time Goethe does not content himself with merely invoking the name of the author who is so precious to both of them. Rather, he makes us hear Ossian as mediated through Werther's words. The result is an outburst of unrestrained emotion, to which both of them succumb, and it is without equal in the novel:

Her senses were in turmoil, she squeezed his hands, pressed them against her breast, she bent forward with a melancholy movement towards him, and their glowing cheeks touched. The world faded from their mind. He flung his arms around her, pressed her to him, and covered her trembling, stammering lips with furious kisses.

For a brief moment, under the impact of Ossian's voluptuous melancholy, all restraint is thrown to the winds and Werther and Lotte admit to a shared need for each other. (The fact that neither Werther nor Lotte – nor Goethe – could have known at the time that Ossian was a forgery – that James Macpherson did not, as he claimed, edit these bardic songs but wrote them himself – may add a certain critical piquancy to the scene; but it in no way diminishes the release of emotions that Werther's reading calls forth at this moment.) Ossian's poetry was a feature of contemporary literary taste; and Goethe captures the particular flavour of the age, one in which certain books could convert their readers into communities of believers. We will recall this moment, when, in the closing two pages of the novel, we discover that Werther commits suicide with Lessing's *Emilia Galotti* open on the table before him. Moreover, we shall have occasion to think back to these issues when we examine the tumultuous reception which Goethe's novel was accorded. *Werther* belongs to a culture in which literature exercised such a powerful hold on the contemporary imagination that it produced 'cult books'. And, in its time, *Werther* became one of the 'cult books' of the age.

No discussion of Werther's relationship to literature would be complete without a consideration of his allusions to the Bible. It is here that, for many readers, the critical perspective on Werther operates with particular force – if for no other reason than that we all have some knowledge of the biblical stories, and can therefore form a view of the appropriateness (or otherwise) of Werther's attempt to establish a kinship between his experience and that of biblical figures. But, while we may abhor Werther's posturing here, we must remember the extent to which, in the age of sentimentalism, the religious life was intimately associated with the emotional (or, as we would put it nowadays, the psychological) life. Where we as modern readers make distinctions, the culture of 'Empfindsamkeit' did not.

In the letter of 15 November (Book Two) Werther reflects on his relationship to religion. He acknowledges that Christ promised help and comfort to those who followed Him. And he wonders if he is not doing God's will by and through his own suffering: 'Did not the son of God himself say that those would be around him whom his father had given him? But if I am not given to him? What if the father wishes to keep me for himself, as my heart says?' (The reference here is to St John, 7, 65 – 'no man can come unto me, except it were given unto him of my Father'). Frequently Werther sees himself not so much as a follower of Christ but as a Christ-like figure himself, as a further sacrificial intermediary between God and the world. The self-stylization that this entails becomes evident in the same letter: 'And if the cup which God asks heaven to put to his human lips tastes bitter, why should I claim more for myself and pretend that it tastes sweet?' The allusion is to St Matthew 26, 39 where Christ prays: 'O my father, if it be possible, let this cup pass from me: nevertheless not as I will but as thou wilt.' Werther's letter culminates in a literal quotation from St Matthew 27, 46 – 'My God, my God, why hast thou forsaken me?' The reference to the 'cup' recurs again later in the novel – for example, in Werther's final letter which is headed 'after eleven' – 'I do not tremble to grasp the cold, terrible cup from which I am to drink the transport of death. You have given it to me: I do not hesitate.' The allusion here is to St John 18, 11, which at this point in the Passion story differs from the synoptic gospels in that it shows Christ as welcoming the cup: 'The cup which my Father hath given me, shall I not drink it?' Werther too welcomes the cup, and he does so in a moment which exemplifies very powerfully the working of the secularized imagination: for in the gospel story it is God who sends the cup, but in Werther's last letter it is Lotte who demands this sacrifice. And the notion of sacrifice is never far from Werther's mind in the last hours of his life. After the scene in which he reads Ossian aloud, he writes the following words to Lotte: 'I shall go ahead, I go to my father, to your father', which echoes St John 14, 28 – 'Ye have heard how I said unto you, I go away, and come again unto you. If ye loved me, ye would rejoice, because I said, I go unto the Father.' Increasingly, as Werther's thoughts turn to death, he insists that his death will have mediating – indeed redemptive – force. Yet it is difficult not to see these multiple references as anything other than desperate attempts at self-justification. Time and time again Werther invests the motif of 'seeing one another again' with transcendental significance, thereby invoking an after-life that will justify him by including him in the select company of those that qualify for resurrection.

A number of Werther's theological references are wilful in their relationship to the biblical originals. The most striking example is to be found in the letter of 30 November from Book Two. There, in the concluding paragraph, Werther imagines himself returning to his father, falling about his neck, and saying: 'I have come again, my father. Do not scold me that I have broken off the wandering which I, in accordance with your will, should endure longer . . . I know only happiness where you are, and before your face I will suffer and rejoice.' And Werther ends this story of the son's return with the words: 'And you, heavenly father, should you send him away?' The echoes of the parable of the prodigal son are manifest. But those echoes point up a contrast (rather than a similarity) between the biblical narrative and Werther's story. In St Luke, 15, 11–32, it is the son who chooses to leave the father; when he returns to the father, the latter rejoices and kills the fatted calf – he does not turn the son away. What St Luke offers us is an illustration of the enduring love and compassion of the father; Werther's 'father' is a withdrawn figure, one who, so it seems, decrees suffering for the son. In Werther's tale there is no equivalent to the father's rejoicing that the lost son has been found, that he who had been dead now lives.

Once again we find ourselves adopting a critical attitude towards Werther. The novel is remarkable for the many and varied ways in which it sustains a view of the main character which never lets us forget that we are witnessing a process of irreversible psychological and spiritual decline. And the point must be made that, despite his frequent attempts at self-justification, Werther has constant flashes of perception and honesty in which he sees the doom that irrevocably threatens him. In the letter of 13 May (Book One) he pictures himself cradling his heart 'like a sick child' – and the motif of sickness recurs throughout the letters. To see Werther as naive, as incapable of questioning himself and his motives, would be profoundly wrong. Often Werther offers us formulations of his own condition that are remarkable in their honesty and precision. In the letter of 22 May (Book One) he speaks of his need to turn in on himself:

I turn back into myself and find a world! Once again, more in vague premonition, in obscure longing, than in precise depiction and vital energy. And then everything swims before my senses and I smile my way dreamily into the world.

Here Werther himself comes close to perceiving that the attempt to supplant the outer world by an inner one of his own making entails a loss of perceptual energy, a condition of partial living. In the letter of 16 July (Book One) he reproaches himself with his fantasies of kissing Lotte, and in horror asks himself if he would be capable of destroying her peace of mind. He concludes: 'no, my heart is not sufficiently depraved! But weak, weak enough! – and is that not depravity?' The moral reckoning here is stern and clear-sighted. Equally, he is on occasion able to recognize the integrity and decency of the people with whom he is most frequently in contact: 'It is true, if my sickness could be healed, these people would do it' (28 August, Book One). The letter of 30 August (Book One) is forthright in its perception of the havoc which the obsession with Lotte brings in its train:

Unhappy man! Are you not a fool? Are you not deceiving yourself? What is the point of this raging, endless passion? I have no prayer other than her; my imagination registers only her shape, and I see everything in the world around me only in relationship with her.

It is noteworthy that this passage begins with Werther addressing himself in the second person: he attempts to stand back, to observe himself from the outside – and to condemn the aberration that holds him in thrall. But not for long. One notes the incredulity and despair in the final sentence – the anguished, near-tautological force of 'alles in der Welt um mich her' (everything in the world around me), and the subtle modulation in the phrase 'im Verhältnisse mit ihr' (in relationship with her). What one expects is the preposition 'zu' (to). But Werther knows the scale of his obsession. He has passed beyond the stage of simply seeing everything in relationship *to* Lotte: rather, his love so possesses him that everything becomes part of the all-consuming love affair *with* ('Verhältnis *mit*') Lotte. In the course of these few sentences Werther's attempt to stand back from his ravaged self collapses. The 'du' (you) of self-admonition gives place to the experiencing 'ich' (I). In a series of lengthy impassioned sentences he reports his helpless dependence on Lotte. Yet the memories bring little comfort, and the few brief sentences that arrest the excited flow of his speech are savage – 'Wilhelm, I often do not know whether I am in the world.' The letter ends with the laconic bitterness of 'I see no end to this misery but the grave.' In such moments Werther expresses the appalling entrapment of a fine and sensitive mind in experiences that promise nothing but doom. And that mind is powerless to halt the vicious downward spiral on which it is embarked. As a psychological study, *Werther* is remarkable for the subtlety and power with which it charts emotional decline. Even for us as modern readers, the letters have lost none of their painfulness. Some of them – particularly the later ones – are ugly in the emotional blackmail and self-centredness. That ugliness is part of their truthfulness.

The letters of Book Two bear witness to every painful, fitful impulse of this decline into pathology. Increasingly we have the sense that letter writing, for Werther, forfeits any cathartic function that it may initially have had. It is almost as though he writes himself into a selfhood that can only exist within its own claustrophobic discourse – writing is the one life of which he is capable. And, heartbreakingly, even that discourse begins to disintegrate. In his autobiography *Poetry and Truth* Goethe comments on the peculiar psychological truth of the letter as the precipitate of the encapsulated self:

Every ill humour is born of, and nurtured by, loneliness. Whoever surrenders to it flees all contradictory voices, and what could be more of a contradiction than good company? That other people rejoice in living is an embarrassment and reproach to such a person, and hence he is driven back into himself by what should take him out of himself. Should he wish to express himself at any time, this will happen in letters. For no one can directly confront a written outpouring, whether happy or miserable. An answer that consists of counter-arguments, however, gives the lonely person the opportunity to confirm himself in his fancies, to acquire even greater obstinacy of spirit.

Goethe goes on to make the point that in Werther's letters the dialogue element becomes narrowed down to one recipient

(Wilhelm). What we hear is really a monologue, and the isolation grows deeper as the novel advances.

The rebuff at court, which is reported at the opening of Book Two, produces a sharp decline in Werther's mood. The letters that report his pain and resentment are extensive and impassioned. And then, on the 16 June, Werther writes:

Yes truly I am only a wanderer, a pilgrim on the earth!
Are you more?

The final sentence is couched in the plural ('Seid ihr denn mehr?'). We cannot be sure who the 'you' are whom Werther addresses. Perhaps the question is directed at humanity in general. These two sentences strike us as being less a letter than a diary entry. They are an outburst, a cry. And this frantic mode becomes more and more prevalent in the second book of the novel. Not even the return to Wahlheim can halt the process of disintegration to which they bear witness. For Werther finds Wahlheim much changed: his beloved walnut trees round the vicarage have been felled (letter of 15 September); Lotte is married to Albert; the family which was expecting an inheritance faces ruin. Moreover, Werther meets the madman who was employed by Lotte's father, and he learns of the crime committed by the 'Bauernbursch'. In both cases Werther identifies with these figures because they have been destroyed by love. Frequently the letters become brief, painful notes, frantic jottings (see the entries, one can hardly call them letters any more, of 3 September, 30 October, 22 November). Once the editor takes over the narration, these fragments are incorporated into his account, often undated.

On several revealing occasions Werther is driven to lament that language loses its purchase on his experience. On 10 October he writes: 'what irritates me is that Albert does not seem to be so happy as he – hoped – as I – believed myself to be – when – I do not like putting dashes, but here I cannot express myself any other way – and it seems to me it is clear enough.' In one sense we must, of course, agree with Werther that what he writes here is most certainly 'clear enough'. But equally, we perceive that Werther's thoughts, if carried to their logical (and emotional) conclusion, would yield statements that are, at the very least, debatable – if not untenable. Similarly, in one of the last letters that Werther writes to Lotte, we witness him repeatedly recoiling from the truth-telling implications of language. He begins his letter

for the last time, then, for the last time I open these eyes . . . This is the last morning. The last! Lotte, I have no feeling for the word 'the last' . . . to die! What does that mean? Still mine, yours! yours, oh beloved! And for one moment – parted, separated – perhaps for ever? No, Lotte, no – How can I expire? How can you expire? We *are*, after all! – To expire! – What does that mean? That is once again a word, an empty sound, without resonance for my heart. – –

In this passage, and it is one of the most painful in the whole novel, Werther tries to un-think the thoughts entailed by his impending suicide. Yet, in a curious way, it is language that is emotionally honest, and Werther has to retreat before its very ruthlessness. Pitifully, he seeks to resist the one experiential truth left to him, a truth housed in the medium that has promised, but now ultimately denies him, mastery. At the end, even language defeats his wish to dictate to the experiential world. Both in Werther's relationship to language and in his use of language, the novel obliges us to recognize his decline for the ugly thing that it is.

Hitherto, I have been concerned to see *Werther* as essentially the psychological study of one particular individual. And I have suggested that, in so far as we view the novel under this aspect, we will find ourselves adopting a critical perspective on Werther: the various themes and concerns we have charted – nature, love, art, religion, language – have all conspired to illuminate the increasing self-encapsulation of Werther's mind. And, while the novel clearly demands from us an acknowledgment of the range and energy of the protagonist's sensibility, yet it also demands that we register as sickness the solipsism that destroys that sensibility from within.

At one crucial point in the novel (perhaps it is even its turning point) Werther interacts with society. It is to that aspect that I now wish to turn – not least because it may help to redress what may have seemed an imbalance in the argument so far. Whereas the psychological issue provides us essentially with a critique of Werther, the novel's social dimension gives us a sense that, however imperfectly focussed Werther's disparagement of the outer world may be, there is yet a measure of justification for some of his responses. As I have already suggested, Werther's is in many ways an unaccommodated sensibility. We may understand that category in existential terms and argue that Werther cannot accept the limitations and constraints of human experience in general; but we must also understand the term 'unaccommodated' in its social sense. For both Werther's sensibility and the world in which he finds himself ('die Welt um mich her', to quote one of his favourite expressions) bear the imprint of a particular historical age. That a Werther is – and feels himself increasingly to be – solitary may tell us something about the social roles that are available to him. None of which is to say that the world is 'wrong' and Werther is 'right'. But it is at the very least to remind us that *Werther*, like all great literature, both belongs to its own age and transcends it.

(d) Werther and society

The first, and most obvious, difficulty which arises in any attempt to discuss Werther's relationship to society has to do with the fact that the novel does not concern itself in any sustained or thorough-going way with social particulars. Now there is a familiar solution to this kind of problem (and it recurs most frequently in Marxist criticism): it consists, quite simply, in the assertion that the lack of evidence also constitutes evidence. The argument would run roughly as follows: because Werther is only imperfectly aware of the social causes of so much of his malaise, he is the victim of that characteristically bourgeois thinking which transposes social issues into issues of metaphysics and psychology (or even psychopathology). But to follow this path is to subscribe to an article of faith which easily becomes indiscriminate. If both the presence of evidence and the absence of evidence are equally convincing 'proofs' of the case being advanced, then the differences between one literary work and another simply evaporate before an all-embracing doctrine in which everything is grist to the ideological mill.

It is surely more helpful to begin with the evidence that is available to us from the novel itself. There are several occasions on which Werther spells out the kind of society in which he feels most at home. In the letter of 12 May (Book One) he describes himself sitting by the well: 'then the girls come from the town and draw water, the most harmless and most necessary of activities, which in days gone by the daughters of kings performed themselves. When I sit there the patriarchal idea comes intensely alive around me.' In one sense, one could argue that Werther is succumbing to sentimentality in such passages. And there have been stern critical voices that have taken him to task for aestheticizing these humble lives, for failing to see the drudgery and deprivation that is inseparable from their social experience. Yet I think we can dispense with such ideological huffings and puffings: not least because a few lines later Werther does reflect on class differences and on the illegitimate restrictions of humanity which they entail:

The humble people of the area already know me and love me, especially the children. I have made one sad observation. When initially I joined them and inquired in a friendly manner about this or that, some of them thought I was making fun of them and answered with hostility. I was not put off by this. But I did feel most strongly what I have already observed: people of some social standing will always maintain a cold detachment from simple people, as though they feared they would lose by any proximity . . .

I know full well that we are not equal, nor can we be so. But I hold the view that whoever believes that he has to keep his distance from the so-called rabble in order to maintain his respect is as reprehensible as the cowardly man who hides from his enemy because he is afraid of being defeated.   (May 15)

Admittedly, the sentiments expressed here are not those of a budding revolutionary: Werther does not offer a social or political programme. But even so, his responses are neither naive nor self-congratulatory. Moreover, he does identify the loss of community as part of his problematic condition: however imperfectly, he is aware that the intensity of his inner life exacts a price – that of forfeiting the society of his fellow man. Granted, he may, in his relationship to the common

people, create a series of idyllic images which function more as
balm to his troubled soul than as any genuine contribution to
the well-being of those who gather at the well. But equally,
Werther does register, and is offended by, the inequalities in the
society around him.

The letter of 26 May (Book One) offers a sharp diagnosis of
particular ways in which modern society does violence to the
promptings of human nature. Werther writes in praise of
nature, in praise of the wholeness of feeling which is present
when men and women heed the demands of their hearts. He
imagines a young man whose love for a girl is so overwhelming
that he devotes himself completely to her. But such a scale of
emotional commitment is socially unacceptable. And Werther
imagines the following scene:

And then along would come a philistine, a man who holds some public
office, and he would say: 'My fine young man! To love is human, only
you must love within human bounds. Divide up your time, some for
work, and the leisure hours you should devote to your girl. Calculate
your fortune, and what remains over after the necessities have been
covered can – with no objection on my part – be used to give her a
present, but not too often, perhaps on her birthday or name day etc.' If
he follows this advice, he will be a serviceable young man, and I will
advise any prince to give him a teaching post. Only – that will be an end
to his love and, if he is an artist, to his art.

At first sight it might seem that Werther here draws a simple
caricature of the philistine with his doctrine of 'moderation in
all things'. But implicit in Werther's statement is the outrage at
any attempt to compartmentalize human beings, to separate
the workaday self from the emotional self, to divide the totality
of the human being. Werther here registers and reacts against
what we – in the wake of Marx – have come to know as the
division of labour. But before Marx, both Goethe and Schiller
perceived that the increasing specialization of modern life
tended to sunder the human personality into separate,
'specialized' units – just as work itself became subdivided into
discrete processes which denied the individual the craftsman's
sense of making a whole object. I am not, of course, claiming
that Werther in this letter emerges as a precocious critic of the
ills of capitalism. But what gives both dignity and authority to

all the rhetoric about 'feeling' and 'nature' is his legitimate sense that in the modern world outrage is being done to the living substance of man.

Such perceptions of cultural malaise inform those sections of the novel in which Werther's experience of society is manifestly in the foreground. The second book opens with Werther's arrival at court, and the letters which span the period from 20 October 1771 to 11 June 1772 chronicle his attempt to pursue an administrative career with one of the legations. The attempt is short-lived. But it is important to note two things: first, Werther's initial response to administrative work is by no means entirely negative (his abandonment of his career is therefore no simple foregone conclusion); secondly, while we may find ourselves arguing that Werther's reaction to the offence he receives is excessive, his perception of the mean-spiritedness of life in diplomatic circles is often uncomfortably acute. The offence done to him is real, and his outrage is not an exercise in facile self-pity.

In the letter of 26 November Werther writes that he is beginning 'to feel quite tolerable here'. Whereas he had earlier (in the letter of 20 July, Book One) disparaged his mother's notion that practical activity would be good for him, he now concedes that he welcomes having something to do – 'the best thing is that there is enough to do'. He also speaks warmly of Count C . . . who is, it seems, not only someone of real intellectual substance but also a man of great warmth and personal charm. The ambassador is, unfortunately, very different: Werther resents his small-mindedness and his linguistic pedantry – 'no "and", no conjunction may be left hanging, and he is the mortal enemy of all inversions which sometimes slip from my pen' (24 December). Werther is, as we know from his letters, fond of using inversion for emphasis (e.g. in the letter of 27 May from Book One – 'much trouble has it cost me to assuage the mother's anxiety'). Unfortunately, Werther is directly responsible to the ambassador, and his irritation mounts daily. He laments the 'glittering wretchedness, the boredom in the midst of the shabby people', and he goes on to offer a bitter portrait of a snobbish woman, the daughter of an

administrative secretary, who talks ceaselessly of her aristocratic birth and her estates. And he detests the social
climbing that is everywhere apparent:

What irritates me most are the wretched circumstances of bourgeois
society. Of course I know as well as anybody how necessary differences
in rank are, and how many advantages I gain from them. But they
should not be an obstacle where I could enjoy a little happiness, a
shimmer of joy.

We are reminded of his comment at the beginning of the novel
where he speaks of his delight at being in the company of
humble people. There too he does not resort to simple
assertions that everybody must become part of one great
family: there as here he bitterly resents the ways in which class
barriers needlessly prevent the free flow of human affection and
good will. It is from this basis of outrage that Werther
frequently derives his biting pen-portraits of ridiculous figures
from the social world. Here is his description of the aunt of Miss
von B . . .:

The dear aunt in her old age lacks everything: she has no decent
finances, no wit, no support other than the line of her forefathers, no
protection other than the class behind which she barricades herself,
and no pleasure other than looking from her upper floor over the
bourgeois heads below.   (24 December)

Werther's sketches are remarkable in their satirical energy. And
what vibrates behind them is more than spleen or pique: on
occasion he sees the full falsity of the frantic scrabbling for
social rank. The letter of 8 January is a particularly good
example:

What kind of people are these whose entire soul is based on
ceremonial, whose every effort and quest is devoted to the end of
moving one place higher at table! . . .
    The fools, who do not see that the place is not important, and that he
who has the first one so rarely plays the leading role! How many a king
is ruled by his minister, how many a minister is ruled by his secretary!
And who then is the first? The man, it seems to me, who can oversee all
the others and who has enough power or cunning to yoke their energies
and passions to the execution of his plans.

One does not need to invoke Hegel's argument about the interdependence of master and slave mentality in the *Phenomenology of Mind* to feel the acuteness and perception of Werther's diagnosis here. The vision of social ambition as a chain of mutually confirming spheres of authority and dependence is remarkable in its cogency and vigour.

Not that this means that Werther himself is proof against the mechanism which he so trenchantly diagnoses. When he commits the social offence of staying too long at table until he is the only commoner left, he manages to extricate himself from the predicament with good grace. But later, when he discovers that he is being talked about, his shame and anger know no bounds. He senses that those who have resented his success rejoice, and he can find no reserves of independence to keep at bay the insidiousness of their malicious gossip:

One can say all one likes about independence, I would like to see the man who can tolerate that rogues talk about him when they have the advantage of him; when their gossip is empty, then one can leave them to it.

This is a revealing passage; for it suggests that Werther has in some measure become part of the pecking order of life in the diplomatic service – in the sense that he cannot answer the wagging tongues with any values that derive from his sense of his own professional worth. Miss von B . . . (who is clearly drawn to Werther) defends him against her aunt's delight in his discomfiture. But not even her advocacy helps: because Werther, with part of his self, acknowledges the mechanisms against which he has offended.

His withdrawal from court is final and irrevocable. And one feels that the disappointment and shame continue to haunt him although they remain largely unspoken. Certainly, after the debacle at court his despairing moods increase. There is, however, one moment in that ever-deepening darkness when we hear an echo of Werther's brief career as a diplomat. When he writes to Albert and requests the loan of his pistols, he does so in the following terms: 'Would you be kind enough to loan me your pistols on a journey which I propose to make? Fare you well!' The letter is horrifying in its double meaning: the journey

which is mentioned is a journey into death, the 'fare you well' –
'Leben Sie recht wohl' – is an injunction to the survivors. Yet
the tone is correct, even slightly stilted and bureaucratic. The
irony resides in the discrepancy between the catastrophic sub-
text and the social normality of the tone. The gap between inner
and outer man could hardly be greater. Werther's last formal
contact with the world he is determined to leave is couched in
the world's own discourse – and it is one that he has not used for
months and that he will never use again. His experiences at
court have made it abundantly clear why he will not and cannot
continue to live in a world that has so little room for his kind of
language and sensibility.

One footnote must be added to Werther's last bureaucratic
communication with Albert. The text of this note is modelled
closely on the letter in which Jerusalem asked to borrow the
pistols with which he shot himself. Jerusalem wrote that letter
to none other than Christian Kestner, the husband of Lotte
Buff, and the 'real life original' of Albert. At Goethe's request,
Kestner wrote a lengthy account of Jerusalem's suicide, and in
it he quoted the text of Jerusalem's letter about the pistols.
Werther writes to Albert:

Wollten Sie mir wohl zu einer vorhabenden Reise Ihre Pistolen leihen?
Leben Sie recht wohl!

And Jerusalem, when he asked to borrow Christian Kestner's
pistols, wrote the following:

Dürfte ich Ew. Wohlgeb. wohl zu einer vorhabenden Reise um ihre
Pistolen gehorsamst ersuchen?

Jerusalem's letter was dated 'October 29 1772, one o'clock in
the afternoon'. Kestner, as the recipient of the letter, was, of
course, able to quote it verbatim in his written account to
Goethe. But Goethe was already in possession of the letter:
when he visited Wetzlar from 6 November to 11 November
1772, he took the letter with him. And it was only some ten days
later that he asked Kestner to let him have a written account of
Jerusalem's death. Jerusalem's letter is even more formal than
Werther's to Albert. This is only to be expected, because there

had been no great closeness between Jerusalem and Kestner. Goethe modifies the original: Werther could hardly address Albert as 'your honour' ('Ew. Wohlgeb.'), or add the adverb 'gehorsamst' (most obediently). But Goethe is careful to keep as much of the bureaucratic tone as is consistent with verisimilitude – the 'Sie' form, the polite intensifier 'wohl', the strange gerund 'vorhabend'. When we read Werther's note in the context of those anguished final letters, the formal tone hits us like a thunderbolt. The language itself enacts the gulf that has opened up between Werther and those kinds of social activity that are available to him. Clearly Goethe was fascinated by the commingling of the bureaucratic and the catastrophic in Jerusalem's letter to Kestner, and he took the letter with him because he sensed that he would use it later.

What, then, are we to make of the social implications of Goethe's novel? We have seen that, however much *Werther* may be a harrowing exploration of the complexities of human nature, it is also explicitly anchored in a particular historical context. In discussing the growth of 'Empfindsamkeit' and Pietism in eighteenth-century Germany, I sought to suggest that both the character and the linguistic mode of Werther's inwardness belong to these broader cultural currents. And in considering the references to society in the novel, we saw that Werther's sickness is manifestly linked to a social situation in which the only career that beckons to him – that of joining the complex judicial and administrative machinery of the Holy Roman Empire – cannot channel his energies and give them a (to him) worthy practical outlet.

When Werther commits suicide, there is on the table in his room a copy of Lessing's play *Emilia Galotti*. We know that Werther has tidied his papers; he must, therefore, have chosen to have Lessing's play with him, and its placing, open on the desk, makes it almost a testament to those who will discover the suicide (and it is by no means the only piece of stage-management in which he indulges). But a testament to what? In that play Lessing transposes to an Italian setting the conflicts of the age and society in which *Werther* appears (the play was first performed in 1772). Lessing is concerned to contrast the immorality and mendacity of the absolutist petty court with the emotional and moral integrity of the bourgeois-patrician family. But Emilia, the daughter of that family, is afraid of the promptings of her own sexuality, afraid that, if she is exposed to the pleasures of court life, she will betray the values that she holds dear; and she implores her father to kill her. Werther too, as we have seen, feels that his emotional and moral substance is being daily eroded by life at court. In this sense, both he and Emilia, for all their differences in temperament and social experience, share a social destiny. The presence of Lessing's play reminded contemporary readers – and reminds us – that Werther's emotional lability and willed death express not simply psychological concerns (the flaw in one young man's temperament) but also larger socio-historical processes.

The extraordinary success of *Werther* implies that this seemingly so private novel captured the mood and aspiration of a whole generation. A comparison with a much more recent phenomenon can serve to clarify the point. As I write (in October 1985) British newspapers and television are full of tributes to James Dean, who was killed in a car crash thirty years ago. Dean became a symbol for the young people of his generation: more than that, he became a cult figure who inspired extraordinary veneration among his followers – it was even reported that bits of his ruined car were cherished as sacred relics. In his major films Dean portrayed the discontented youth who, like Werther, is, in both senses of the term, a 'rebel without a cause' (to quote the title of one of Dean's best-known films): a rebel who is not aware of a particular cause that would justify his rebellion (the Dean figure is not economically or socially disadvantaged); and a rebel who has no positive social or political cause for which he can fight (the Campaign for Nuclear Disarmament, the Students' Rebellion as points of focus for the discontent of young people all come after Dean's death). Dean expressed the unease of a generation that felt dissatisfied, that felt it had been denied an outlet for its energies. His motto 'live fast, die young, have a beautiful corpse' has more than a few echoes of *Werther*.

The difference in aesthetic quality between Goethe's *Werther* and Dean's films is enormous. The point of drawing the comparison is not, therefore, to equate the two as pieces of imaginative creation: but I offer it as evidence that when whole groups of people dressed like Werther (with the short boots, the blue frock coat, the yellow waistcoat) or like James Dean, this was more than one of the many vagaries of fashion. A fictional persona was being confirmed in its social truthfulness. Werther and James Dean were truthful to the 1770s and the 1950s in that they captured a climate in which young people felt within themselves energies which, denied any practical outlet, became self-destructive.

(e) Recounting and reflecting

In discussing Werther's relationship to society I have had occasion to remark on the sharpness and linguistic energy of his critical perceptions. The burden of such an argument has, I think, important implications for our understanding of the novel as a whole, because it suggests that, at certain times, Werther's discourse detaches itself from the questionable (psychological) context of its making and stands in its own right by virtue of its sheer human truthfulness. In other words: it does not matter who writes these statements, because we recognize their value and truth on the basis of our shared experience. The discourse has a force and cogency that transcends its source in the particular psychological state of Werther. The distinction between Werther's discourse as the expression of a particular individuated self and Werther's discourse as an irreducibly perceptive illumination of human affairs is one that we must constantly bear in mind. We can hear this distinction in the enthusiastic response to the novel which was recorded by Ludwig Tieck: writing in 1828, years after its first appearance, he recalls the impact *Werther* made on him as a young man:

I was seventeen years old when *Werther* appeared. For four weeks I was bathed in tears, which I shed not for the love and not for the fate of poor Werther but in anguish of the heart – in the humiliating consciousness that I did not think this way, that I could not be like this man. I was overcome by the idea that whoever is able to perceive the world as it really is must think in this way.

Tieck expresses more than heady enthusiasm, more than simple identification with Werther (and, as we shall see later, there was no shortage of voices that did that). Tieck's enthusiasm for the novel was directed not at its psychological accuracy, nor at its story of doomed love. Rather, he was overwhelmed by the truth of what Werther wrote and perceived, by the sense that Werther's discourse was a revelation of man's being in the world. In other words, for the young Tieck, *Werther* was a philosophical rather than a psychological novel.

How are we to separate the psychological from the philosophical issue? Are there features of the text itself which invite us to do this? Or is it simply that we as readers will heed the promptings of our own dispositions (those who respond psychologically will see the novel as a remarkable study of a complex personality, those who are of a more philosophical turn of mind will see the novel as exploring certain dilemmas that are part of man's essential human endowment)? I think that the text does, at a number of crucial points, make clear that we are being asked to acknowledge two kinds of appeal to two kinds of human truth. These appeals are interrelated in as much as they derive from one source (Werther, the writer of the letters); but in their import for us they are ultimately distinct.

The following five quotations will help to establish this point. In the letter of 17 May (Book One) Werther begins with three paragraphs of general reflections on the lot of humankind, and then goes on to describe in vivid detail some of the people whose acquaintance he has made. He ends the letter with an intriguing sentence in which he presumably refers to the narrative energy he has just displayed: 'Fare well! The letter will please you, it is largely historical.'

My second passage comes from the letter of 16 June (Book One); a crucial letter, because it describes Werther's first meeting with Lotte. In the first paragraph he announces that he has got to know somebody who touches his heart; and he continues:

To tell you the sequence of events by which I got to know one of the most delightful of creatures will not be easy. I am contented and happy and, as a result, I am not a good storyteller [Historienschreiber].

An angel! – Rubbish! Everybody says that of the people near to them, don't they? And yet I am not able to explain to you how perfect she is, why she is perfect. Suffice it to say that she has captured all my thoughts.

So much simplicity with so much good sense, so much goodness with so much firmness of character, and her inner calm combined with real life and activity. –

This is all trivial rubbish that I have just said of her – wretched abstractions. Some other time – no, not some other time, I must tell [erzählen] it to you now. If I don't do it now, it will never happen. For, between ourselves, since I began to write to you, I was three times on the point of putting down my pen, having my horse saddled, and riding out. And yet I promised myself this morning not to ride out, but I keep on going to the window to see how high the sun is in the sky. – –

I could not restrain myself, I had to go and see her. Here I am again, Wilhelm, eating my supper in the evening and writing to you. What bliss it is to my soul to see her in the circle of the sweet, lively children, her eight brothers and sisters! –

If I go on like this, you will be no clearer than you were at the beginning. So listen, I will force myself to go into details.

This is a wonderfully vivid passage in the original, and I can only hope that my translation has not drained it of its vigour. Werther is trying to convey to Wilhelm an experience of the greatest importance. And the passage is shot through with the opposition between saying ('sagen') and recounting ('erzählen'). It is difficult to capture this contrast in English, because the verb 'recount' sounds so formal and stilted. But Werther finds himself caught between two contradictory impulses: between *saying* what Lotte means to him, how beautiful and captivating she is, and *recounting* the sequence of events which brought them together. Both strike him as inadequate: to enthuse about her is to indulge in 'abstractions' ('simplicity', 'good sense', 'inner calm' and so on), yet to tell the story is to offer but a pale reflection of her true beauty of heart and mind. Moreover, to tell the story, to recount the events, strikes Werther as less satisfactory than experiencing directly. For this reason he breaks off his letter. We are to realize that there is an interruption of several hours between paragraphs four and five. Werther becomes restless at his table, he goes constantly to the window, and finally he rides off to see Lotte. He only resumes his letter in the evening. And then, at long last, he does give

Wilhelm the details of how he actually met Lotte ('ins Detail gehen').

My third passage comes from the very next letter (19 June). It opens: 'how far I got with my story [Erzählung] I don't know any more; I do know that it was two in the morning when I went to bed . . . What happened on our return from the dance I have not yet recounted [erzählt], and today is not the day for it.' Despite his disclaimer, Werther then goes on to offer a brief narrative of their return to Lotte's home. He closes the letter of 19 June with the following words: 'since then the sun, the moon, and the stars can happily continue with their cycle, I do not know whether it is day or night, and the whole world goes blurred around me'. Werther's bliss is so intense that he loses any sense of linear time, he is oblivious to the familiar cycle of day and night.

The fourth passage comes from the second book of the novel. The letter of 15 March, like the ones we have just examined, also reports a decisive experience. But in this case, it is a hurtful one – Werther's humiliation at court. The letter begins with a furious outburst:

I have received a hurt that will drive me away from here. I gnash my teeth! To Hell! It cannot be made good, and you alone are all to blame, you who urged me, drove me, tormented me to take on a job that did not suit me. Now I am landed with the consequences! Now you are landed with the consequences! And just so you cannot say that my overheated ideas have ruined everything, my dear sir, I shall now give you an account [Erzählung], plain and clear, such as a chronicler would record.

These are, to put it mildly, unattractive sentiments, but they do not concern me here. What is important for my purposes is Werther's invoking of the category of linear narrative as part of his attempt to explicate his experience.

My final passage comes again from the second book of the novel, from the letter of 4 September, in which Werther reports his meeting with the farmhand. He recounts a conversation which he has had with the young man. He then breaks off with the following exclamation:

Here, oh best of friends, I begin my usual lament which I will go on repeating for ever and a day: if only I could represent the man as he stood before me, as he still stands before me! If only I could express [sagen] everything properly so that you would feel how I sympathize, must sympathize with his fate!

Three lines later Werther comments: 'As I read through this page, I see that I have forgotten to tell [erzählen] the end of the story, but it is one that can readily be imagined.'

The foregoing quotations come from different parts of the novel, and they reflect varying moods in Werther. But they all have one thing in common: they draw attention to two different modes of writing, to contrasting (and complementary) facets of the process by which human beings capture their experience in language (in this case, in the written language of the letter). The two modes are: on the one hand that of story-telling, of recounting events in their chronological sequence; and on the other, that of reflection, commentary, discursive analysis. These two modes are instantly familiar, because we ourselves use them all the time as we mingle experience with reflection, story-telling with commentary. Most narrative literature is characterized by a constant and subtle interplay of these two modes. Within first-person narration, the difference between the two can often be felt as a manifest (but rarely watertight) temporal separation: the present, narrating self looks back on his or her past, experiencing self. What happened *then* is interspersed with the comments and reflections of *now*. Clearly, in an epistolary novel such as *Werther* the gap between 'then' and 'now' may be very slight: Werther can, and often does, write in immediate proximity to the events he describes. Sometimes the gap between experiencing and writing closes when Werther, as it were, muses aloud in his letters to Wilhelm. At such moments reflection and experience and writing all flow into one another.

Yet, however much Werther might wish to live his life in this kind of unitary state – the state where reflecting, experiencing, and writing are one – he is not able to prolong the privileged moment. For, like all of us, he is subject to the law of sequential time: he cannot stop the onward flow of experience. Linearity, the law of story-telling, will not be gainsaid. Werther knows, when writing to Wilhelm, that some of his experiences can only be conveyed in the linear mode of the chronological event sequence. In the 16 June letter about the first meeting with Lotte, he realizes that all his statements about her inward qualities necessarily remain abstract, that concreteness can only be found when he tells the story of how he came to meet her. And the same is true of the disaster that ends his administrative career: the crisis is inseparable from certain events that occurred in a knowable sequence: and without an account of these events as they occurred, his expressions of outrage remain blurred and unmotivated.

It is significant (although the fact has often gone unremarked) that Werther is punctilious about dating his letters. We do know the precise span of time which the novel covers (and such precision is altogether rare in epistolary novels). It is only after the editor enters the novel that we find notes and jottings from Werther's pen that are undated. And we register this fact as symptomatic of his decline: the papers, like the life, become so chaotic that the editor has to step in to ensure a measure of narrative clarity. And in this novel, as in so many others, the linear sequence of events is decisive. *Werther* ends with an event that is terrible and final: his death occurs in the outer world, as part of a chronological sequence. The sting of the novel's conclusion is inseparable from its once-and-for-all character.

In its interplay of linear and reflective modes *Werther* both explores the existential significance of these two modes and shows them to be symptomatic of a profound dilemma at the heart of the protagonist's being, a dilemma which has to do with his acute self-consciousness. I shall return to this point later. I give below, in summary form, an indication of what the interrelationship of recounting and reflecting modes achieves in the novel:

First: Because Werther is a young man of introspective temperament, large sections of the letters he writes consist of passages of reflection, analysis, rhapsody in which he comments not only on his own experience but on that of humanity in general.

Second: *Werther* is concerned with a young man who falls in love with a girl whom he cannot marry. After a brief but unsuccessful attempt at a career in the diplomatic service, he succumbs to increasing melancholy and finally takes his own life. In other words, *Werther* tells a story, it recounts events in chronological sequence.

Third: The novel, both in the letters written by the protagonist and in the editor's concluding account, explores the problematic interplay of recounting and reflecting modes.

Fourth: It is this subtle interplay which makes *Werther* the finest and most intelligent of all eighteenth-century epistolary novels. In an earlier chapter we saw how the aesthetic of eighteenth-century epistolary fiction appealed to two quite distinct categories of truthfulness. One was what we might call a 'story telling' principle: the letters, it was asserted, were authentic documents, written by 'real life' people: names were changed (or abbreviated) in order to conceal (but thereby, of course, to invoke) the authentic basis of the experiences recounted. The other was what we might call the 'reflective' principle: the claim was that it did not matter whether the material presented 'really' happened: its truthfulness was to be decided by other criteria – if it was felt to be in accord with the way human beings behave, then it would be true. *Werther* manipulates both these strategies with consummate skill. The factual basis of Werther's doomed love affair is asserted with a specificity of time and place (the editor tells us, in a footnote to the letter of 26 May in Book One, that 'Wahlheim' is an invented name and adds – 'we felt ourselves obliged to alter the true names which appear in the original'). We are persuaded, then, that there is a story, a sequence of events in linear time, which actually occurred. Yet at the same time *Werther* contains many passages of general reflections on the destiny of man: and these are as truthful as we find them to be illuminating perceptions of human experience.

Fifth: In an earlier section I discussed *Werther* as a psychological study. And I was at pains to suggest that, under such an aspect, we find ourselves viewing Werther critically:

that is, we see him as a person whose cast of mind blights his relationships with the world outside him. In advancing such an argument, I was treating Werther as a knowable human being, as somebody who is seen in the context of other human lives, and who is, in consequence, subject to the reader's moral evaluation. This argument depends very heavily on the 'recounting' aspect of the novel: we see Werther's sensibility in the context of his story, of his relationships with his human, social, and natural environment.

Sixth: It is, of course, symptomatic of Werther's sickness that he seeks to live in the inner rather than in the outer world, that he tries to legislate for the outer world by acknowledging it only in so far as it corroborates his feelings and intuitions. He tries, that is, to make the recounting mode match the reflective mode (all of which gives point to the editor's revelations of the mismatches and discrepancies – nowhere more devastatingly than in the account of the botched suicide). Yet at the same time the novel is uncompromising in its demand that we attend to the workings of Werther's inwardness. And I want now to turn to those reflective or rhapsodic passages from Werther's pen which, regardless of their psychological source, uncover and illuminate important reaches of human experience.

I am not thereby urging that we forget the psychological issue; we neither can nor should do that. But any adequate response to Goethe's novel demands that we set alongside the psychological issue the realization that some of what Werther writes, in its linguistic energy and distinction, constitutes an enlargement of our sense of the possibilities of human feeling and cognition. The simple plot of *Werther* is a sad love story, and much of what he writes belongs to that strand. But much of the discourse of Werther's letters is not reducible to that sphere of thematic concern: for Werther's letters make us share in a powerful vision of the splendour and anguish of the kind of human sensibility which is uncompromising in its oscillation between self-consciousness and the demand for fullness and intensity of experience.

(f) The truthful discourse

Because of the existential dilemma which it expresses, *Werther* is more than a story of doomed love: it is a tragedy of the human spirit. It is also, to historicize that argument, the tragedy of a specific historical sensibility. *Werther* bears witness to the glory and the anguish that are part of a particular stage in the emergence of modern, secular individualism. Herbert Schöffler has illuminated this aspect of the novel for us. He points out that the many references to the Bible (and in particular to St John's gospel) make us see Werther's sufferings as a secular Passion. Werther's suicide is symptomatic of an existence without religious security; hence the closing sentence of the novel: 'no clergyman accompanied him'. Schöffler has also taught us to see Ossian as a key work in the history of secular culture: for in Macpherson's 'epic' the lamenting voice of man is constantly answered by an echo: there are no gods in Ossian, there is only the longing for them. The voice that answers man's lament is but his own utterance, magnified as it rebounds from the surfaces of the natural world. Werther, then, is representative of a generation caught between the waning of religious faith (under the impact of the Enlightenment) and the coming of that new kind of secular (that is, historicized) spirituality that would be announced some thirty years later by the German Idealist philosophers (particularly Hegel). Werther finds himself denied the support of religious faith in any conventional sense: but equally he cannot believe that the stuff of human society is no more than matter spiritualized and thereby informed by a higher purpose. His anguished quest for a fullness of experience that is denied him by his self-consciousness makes the hopeless love for Lotte part of a larger, tragic design. When Werther oscillates between what I have called the 'recounting' and the 'reflecting' mode, he thereby expresses one of the deepest sources of his dilemma. For his is a sensibility caught between self-consciousness on the one hand and on the other the need to drown the knowing self in experiences of engulfing intensity. It is the presence of this dilemma which means that *Werther* is concerned with more than simple emotional imbalance. Both

the thoughts that take shape in Werther's self-conscious spirit
and the kinds of experience to which he turns in his quest for
existential integrity make this novel richer than the psychological case study of one particular individual.

Where, then, shall we begin to identify these larger themes?
One answer – and it is an existential rather than historical one –
has been offered by Roland Barthes in his *Fragments d'un
Discours amoureux* (*Fragments of a Discourse of Love*). This is
both a charming and an eccentric work. Its particular interest
for students of *Werther* is twofold: first, Barthes's book is, as it
were, a love affair with Goethe's novel, for references to
Werther recur with great insistence and urgency; second (and
this is the aspect of particular interest in the present context),
Barthes cherishes *Werther* as the paradigm for a love that works
in and through language. Barthes's book gives us little or no
sense of the story which *Werther* tells. The moral issue has no
place in his book; nor does he attempt to give us any indication
of Werther's character or individuated psychology. Instead, the
quotations from Werther's letters function as timeless expressions of the mode of the 'discours amoureux'. Barthes divorces
the discourse from the person, in order to attest the truthfulness
to the human heart which is embodied in that discourse. Two
examples will have to suffice. At one point Barthes writes:

It is a case of (and herein resides the beauty of the book) a tragic
disposition. Werther does not hate Albert; it is simply that Albert
occupies a desired position.   (p. 171)

For Barthes, *Werther* is a novel which explores not the
particular workings of desire as manifested in one individuated
character, but the varying figurations, the flux of desire itself.
To quote him again:

Werther is pure discourse of the loving subject: only once is the
monologue (idyllic, anguished) broken, at the end, shortly before the
suicide.   (p. 244)

What Barthes's book offers, with splendid eloquence, is a
tribute to Werther's uncompromising sensibility: the power of
his discourse quite simply is its truth. Barthes does not concern

himself with Werther's interaction with other people, he does not ask whether the demands he makes on Lotte are justified. Love exists not within the moral parameters of two people's dealings with one another: rather, it is a state of being that has become language. A comment Barthes makes – 'why is it better to *last* than to burn?' (p. 30) – could, we feel, well apply to Werther. Intensity is all. Barthes offers us no detailed interpretative help with *Werther*; but he does express an uncompromising validation of Werther's discourse, and he quite simply takes it for granted that that discourse stands apart from (and is untainted by) the persona of its maker.

It is important to provide the historical context for that truthfulness which Barthes sees in *Werther*. I have frequently had occasion to stress that Werther's letters are couched in the language of sentimentalism ('Empfindsamkeit'). As an example of the style of contemporary letter writing one could take the following which was written to Herder by Lavater in November 1772:

Never before have I felt what I now feel as I sit down to write – to you, my supremely chosen friend. Oh, Providence, knower of the heart, bringer of joy, how carefully have you watched over me! It was not in vain that I trusted in you! . . . Now, friend, I cannot answer – but I must write – and would rather weep – spirit myself away to your side – dissolve – lie on your breast – and take the friends of my heart, two women, with me to you – and even – not say but gaze, touch, breathe: 'You are and we are.'

It is difficult not to feel that a little of this goes a long way. What concerns me chiefly here is the contrast we immediately feel between Lavater's effusion and Werther's letters. By comparison, Werther's prose is terse and muscular; above all, we feel that he means what he writes and writes what he means. It is as though, in his sensibility, the modish diction of 'Empfindsamkeit' is invested with the full engagement of the personality. And this brings us to a crucial fact of Werther's sensibility – his commitment to sincerity of action, feeling, utterance. To repeat the terms I have already employed in discussing Werther's discourse: he seeks at all times to close the gap between recounting and reflecting. He refuses to accept the insufficiency of worldly experience, to live at less than full pressure. And when the outer world does not vouchsafe him adequate experience, he withdraws into himself in order to try and maintain the consonance between experience and consciousness. The price he pays is a terrible one: he loses all hold on the phenomenal world, he loses any sense of the contours that define the self. But what gives even his distraught letters a kind of dignity is the fact that behind all their obsessive rhetoric we can still detect the unabated will to live – and die – in experiential truthfulness, rather than compromise, rather than adjust to a lesser scale of feeling, knowing, and writing.

Much of this territory has been charted by Lionel Trilling's *Sincerity and Authenticity*. In his study Trilling offers a significant piece of cultural history: he traces the differing values that have been ascribed to notions of 'being true to one's self' over the past two-and-a-half centuries. And for him, *Werther* is a cardinal document in that historical sequence. He reminds us that when Goethe discovered Diderot's novel *Le Neveu de Rameau* (*Rameau's Nephew*) in 1803, he immediately recognized its centrality for contemporary culture, and translated it into German. *Rameau's Nephew* was written between 1761 and 1774 (the period of its composition overlaps with that of *Werther*), but it was not published in Diderot's lifetime. It was purchased from Diderot by his patron Catherine the Great, was secretly copied, and found its way to Germany where Goethe and Schiller were immediately seized of its importance. There is, of course, no question of Goethe having known – or even known about – Diderot's novel at the time when he was working on *Werther*. But it is difficult not to believe that the Goethe who read *Rameau's Nephew* recognized it as a counterpart to *Werther*.

Rameau's Nephew consists of a dialogue between an 'I' (a Diderot figure) and the unashamedly eccentric and parasitic musician who is named in the title of the novel. The nephew is richly blessed with the gifts of irony and parody, and he debunks with relish the accepted values of contemporary society. He is an unashamed buffoon and mimic, and his irreverence is contrasted with the decency and good sense of the

Diderot figure. Trilling, in his analysis, draws heavily on, and acknowledges, Hegel's discussion of the novel in his *Phenomenology of Mind*. For Hegel is at pains to see the nephew not simply as some self-indulgent bohemian, but as a protagonist of profound spiritual significance. In Hegel's eyes, the ironist represents a necessary stage in the process of growing self-consciousness which shapes the history of the modern world. For only by passing through the stage of irony (and self-irony) will the human mind find itself and achieve eventual autonomy. The mind must, therefore, have the courage to be true to its own self-estrangement – and must refuse to accept any of the social accommodations available to it. Otherwise it will betray itself and betray the historical progression of which it is the problematic – but necessary – agent.

In many ways, the contrast between the nephew and Werther is very great. Unlike Werther, the nephew does not for a moment lose sight of where his self ends and where the social world begins. Indeed, his mimicry presupposes precisely the ability both to register and to keep at bay the norms of society. What society offers him is roles, roles that are played with knowing, self-conscious relish. Werther is different. He is not prepared to live a role, to go through the motions. For him there is either intensity of feeling, total commitment of the self – that is, sincerity – or there is nothing. Hence his suicide is not merely a psychological aberration: it is the martyrdom of a sensibility that will not, as it were, cut its coat according to the available cloth. Werther always insists on wearing *his* coat. Trilling comments:

[Werther] is in all things the sincere man; even in his disintegration he struggles to be true to the self he must still believe is his own. It is much to the point, especially in the light of Rameau's wild impersonations and role-playings, that Werther expresses his sincerity by a singular and apparently unchanging mode of dress . . . A disintegrated consciousness, he had persisted in clinging to the simplicity of the honest soul.   (p. 52)

But, for all the gulf that separates them, Werther and the nephew are radical enactments of a profound unease within the modern sensibility. Both novels establish a debate between the unaccommodated and the accommodated self: the nephew crosses swords with the Diderot figure; and in *Werther* there is the implicit dialogue between the protagonist and Wilhelm, the recipient of the letters. As we have already seen, the dialogue becomes increasingly a monologue. And this is because Werther lacks the nephew's ability, as ironist, to engage in witty and disrespectful commerce with the world around him. Werther, the would-be 'honest soul', ends up, in one sense, talking to himself. In another sense, of course, this is only partially true. Because, by virtue of the fact that Werther's letters are published by the editor, Werther to the very end remains in a kind of dialogue with the editor – and thus with us, the readers. And in this way Werther's corrosive, self-consuming inwardness becomes a challenge to us. In a way that remains true some two hundred years after its first publication, *Werther* retains its subversive power. It has lost none of its ability to disturb us, to call into question the compromises by which we all live.

Trilling's argument focusses with admirable urgency the ways in which Werther's discourse had an authority and stature that is greater than simple truthfulness to the promptings of individuated psychology. Moreover, Trilling has helped us to see that Werther's sincerity is not a given condition: it is something that he wills, that he demands of himself in answer to the depredations of his self-awareness. Time and time again we hear the renegade voice of knowingness that threatens to blight his experience. Not that Werther is another incarnation of Rameau's nephew: but the basis from which he bends every sinew to be the 'honest soul' is akin to that from which the nephew mounts his barrage of irony. I have already drawn attention to the thematized disjunction in his letters between recounting and reflecting. It is symptomatic of the anguish of a sophisticated temperament, of a mind that generates human aspirations that go beyond the framework of practical living. Lotte's unattainability stands for a much larger issue than the unfortunate timing of Werther's emotional attachments. Werther longs to submerge the knowing self in experiences that will engulf it: but the observing self will not be exorcized.

Much of this surfaces in the very first letter of the novel. The opening sentence twice asserts the 'I am' of individuated selfhood, one that rejoices in its condition of separateness: 'How glad *I am* that *I am* away!' Werther writes to Wilhelm of his bad conscience and asks himself how far he has been guilty of encouraging the affections of the hapless Leonore. He pronounces himself both innocent and guilty, and he then promises Wilhelm that he will abandon his brooding and will try to live with simple integrity in the present:

I will, dear friend, I promise you, I will improve, I will no longer chew over the little disagreeable things which Fate decrees for us, as I have always done; I will enjoy the present and what is past shall be over and done with. Certainly, you are right, oh best of men, there would be less pain in human kind if people did not – God knows why they are made this way – with such energy and imagination concern themselves with keeping alive the memory of past disagreeableness rather than coping with a neutral present. (4 May)

In this letter we hear Werther promising himself to live innocently in the present – without brooding, remembering, reflecting. Yet even as he makes the promise, we know he will not be able to keep it. Four times in a mere two lines he writes 'I will': and the assertiveness comes from the need to silence the refractory self. But the 'Ich' will not mysteriously evaporate, will not become an unproblematic, unreflective entity. Mental life, Werther tells us, is disagreeable. It feeds on – and compounds – unwelcome and troubling experiences: indeed, it is the very medium and agency of experiential dissatisfaction. And Werther indicts one particular faculty as the root of all this disunity: the imagination ('Einbildungskraft'). Yet we feel that Werther can no more dispense with his imagination than he can dispense with the air he breathes. Werther cannot live without making mental pictures of actual (or potential) experience. Even when he responds to what is there before him (a natural scene, a particular person, a group of people), he is not a disinterested spirit, a blank sheet of paper on which the external world leaves a direct, unmediated imprint. His experiencing is inseparable from his picturing of experience. And time and time again that picturing faculty will re-group the simple facts before him, or it will go beyond the observable facts altogether and make alternative images. Werther longs for a harmony between self and world, a totality of being and knowing which admits of no gaps or fissures. But time and time again he will lament that either the physical, palpable world blights the image, or the image blights the physical world.

It is within this kind of dilemma that we can most justly appreciate Werther's oft-repeated longing for the simple life, a longing that is rarely free from an admixture of disparagement. In the letter of 22 May (Book One) Werther writes:

That children do not know why they want certain things is something on which all highly learned schoolmasters and tutors agree. But that adults too, like children, tumble around on this earth and, like them, do not know where they come from and where they are going, that they are as little able to act according to genuine aims, that they are just as much ruled by biscuits, and cakes, and the rod – nobody wants to believe that, but it seems to me that it is patently obvious.

I gladly concede, because I know what you would answer, that those people are the happiest who, like children, live from day to day, who drag their dolls after them, who dress and undress them and who with great respect slink around the drawer in which Mummy keeps the sweets and, when they finally get what they want, munch it with full cheeks and call out 'More!' – They are happy creatures. And those people are also contented who give high-sounding titles to their wretched concerns and even to their passions, and tell all humanity that these are mighty operations devoted to its health and well-being. – Happy the man who can be like that!

This is a magnificent and a devastating passage. In every line we hear the anguish of a spirit that knows not only what it knows but also *that* it knows. And we can be in no doubt that such a spirit will never be able to submerge itself once and for all in integral, unreflective existence.

A mere two pages later, in the letter of 27 May, Werther returns to the praise of simple existence. He meets a young mother and strikes up a brief conversation: and he salutes 'such a creature who follows the narrow circle of her existence, who gets by from one day to the next, who sees the leaves falling and thinks no more of it than that winter is coming'. No intimation of transience or mortality troubles this woman – according to Werther. Yet if such tributes to simple integrity vibrate with an implicit claim to intellectual superiority on Werther's part, there are also remarks in which he ironizes his own pretensions to intellectual sophistication. At the beginning of that same letter, Werther comments on the previous letter in which he had started by describing two children and then drifted off into musings about nature and art. Werther, on re-reading what he has written, adds: 'I have, as I see, been succumbing to transports, parables, and declamation, and in the process I forgot to tell you what happened to the children.' The verb used here is 'auszuerzählen' – Werther forgot to tell his story through to its conclusion. Once again, the opposition between recounting and reflecting ('declaiming') makes itself heard. And when Werther goes on to recount how the mother came to collect the children, he begins: 'I sat, lost in picturesque feeling . . . for fully two hours.' The irony is unmistakable as Werther makes fun of his own pretentiousness. He is aware of the danger that his imagination makes pictures – and may, on occasion, be picturesque and little more. When Marxist critics disparage Werther for making false idylls out of the lives of simple people, they overlook the fact that he is aware of that tendency himself. Granted, that awareness does not ripen into a programme for economic and social reform. And the attraction Werther feels for the humble figures of the village community partakes more of an existential than a social theme (Werther is concerned with modes of existence in which there is no disjunction between experience and reflection). But we should note that Werther does not simply espouse the patronizing stance of the complex self who administers the odd indulgent pat on the head to worthy peasants.

Moreover, as the very next letter makes clear, Werther is himself troubled by his tendency to convert situations into idylls (etymologically, the word 'idyll' means 'little picture'). Werther is unsettled, not by questions of social injustice, but by the fear that his perception may be a distortion of the actuality before his eyes, that consciousness may (once again) betray experience. He writes: 'I witnessed a scene today which, if copied clearly, would have made the loveliest idyll in the world; yet what is the point of literature, scene, and idyll? Must there always be tinkering ['muss es . . . gebosselt sein'] as soon as we are engaged by a natural phenomenon?' Werther is tormented by the limiting factor of his own 'tinkering' selfhood. He despairs of his ability, as artist, ever to capture what is there before him in the outer world.

At one point, in a much later letter – of 24 July, Book One – he imagines that he would be a better copyist if he took clay or wax: then he would be able to reproduce the form of a natural object without the falsifying intrusions of self-consciousness. But he himself realizes that that solution is problematic: 'I imagine that, if I had clay or wax, I would be able to get the outward image right' ('ich bilde mir ein, wenn ich Ton hätte oder Wachs, so wollte ich's wohl herausbilden'). The German is, alas, untranslatable, because it depends on a pun. The German word for 'imagination' is 'Einbildungskraft' – literally: the power of making inner forms or pictures. The verb 'sich einbilden' often has the force of 'imagining falsely', that is 'deluding oneself'. So Werther is deluding himself when he imagines that, with clay or wax, he could find the perfect outward form – 'herausbilden': again the verb 'bilden' occurs, which means 'to shape' or 'to form'. But any 'form' men make with their hands, outwardly, will be dependent on the (perhaps distorted) inner forms of the imagination. That one sentence takes us to the heart of Werther's dilemma. It is a dilemma that embraces not simply questions of artistic verisimilitude and accuracy; for what is at stake is the shaping power of a sophisticated human consciousness, and the extent to which that faculty may be an agency that misshapes the natural world which it so earnestly seeks to know and to cherish.

I have no wish to convert Werther into some kind of austere philosophical deity who wrestles with weighty problems that are more properly the domain of professional philosophers. But what I do wish to suggest is that his claim to be the 'honest soul' only gives us part of the picture of his sensibility. It is important that we see that Werther wages his battle for sincerity against fearsome odds. And these odds are provided not only by the outer world, but by the characteristic cast of his sensibility. Werther is one of the many heroes of European literature since the eighteenth century who have felt their self-consciousness to be the enemy of living, a blight on their ability to find sustenance in the phenomenal world. In the letter of 16 June (Book One) Werther writes a lovely description of Lotte's beauty when she dances:

You have to see her dancing! You see, she is so much at one with the movement, with all her heart and all her soul, her whole body one complete harmony, so carefree, so unselfconscious, as though that were actually everything, as though she were thinking of nothing else, feeling nothing else. And in that moment assuredly everything else fades into insignificance.

The passage celebrates a pattern of grace and movement in which the girl becomes enveloped in a blissful sense of oneness, both mental and physical. Werther's description is a glimpse of a moment of privileged wholeness: it belongs with Kleist's essay *On the Marionette Theatre*, with Rilke's concern in the *New Poems* to celebrate the integral being of plants, animals, objects, with W. B. Yeats's lines:

> O body swayed to music, O brightening glance,
> How can we know the dancer from the dance?

Such moments derive their poignancy from their contrast with the disunited state that is perceived as the usual – perhaps even the necessary – condition of the modern sensibility. In *Werther* the vision of Lotte dancing contrasts with those countless moments when the promise of wholeness is suddenly dashed. A mere six pages later, Werther regrets the blight which befalls his experience because the experiencing agent is a tainted being. He does so in a little parable that would be worthy of Kafka in its manichean condemnation of all physical experience:

A great, twilit wholeness rests before our soul, our feeling, like our eyes, swims and fades in it, and we long, ah, to surrender our whole being to it, to let ourselves be filled with the total bliss of one single, great, splendid feeling. – And alas! when we rush towards it, when the 'there' becomes a 'here', everything is as it was, and we stand in our poverty, in our constriction, and our soul longs for the refreshing draught that has slipped away.

The promise of wholeness is tormentingly vivid: but when the intimation becomes actuality, when the promise becomes reality, when the 'there' becomes the 'here', only disenchantment results. The vision stands revealed as a mere chimera, and insufficiency becomes the ineluctable law of experience. At such moments, Werther joins the ranks of those heroes who are condemned to be onlookers at the dance in which, briefly and magically, a human being recaptures a condition of wholeness in the midst of everything that conspires to fragment and divide modern man.

On frequent occasions we are made to feel that Werther's perception of the lot of man is both impressive and enriching. Not that this is simply to make Werther 'right' and the world 'wrong'. But Goethe's novel demands of us a kind of complicity with its protagonist – even when it stresses his questionableness as an individuated character. On occasion we simply forget who is writing these letters. Their truthfulness stands (or falls) by criteria that have to do with the direct appeal to us, the readers, to share in the perceptions of a radically unprotected sensibility. And there are moments when Werther's comments on the generality of humankind have a force and cogency that will not be gainsaid. In the letter of 17 May (Book One) he writes:

It is a monotonous condition that characterizes the human race. Most of its members consume the greater part of their time in staying alive, and the little remainder of freedom which they have frightens them so much that they look for every means to get rid of it. Oh the destiny of man!

The last phrase rings out with a splendid irony: its grandiloquent gesture contrasts powerfully with the vivid picture of frantic, treadmill existence which precedes it. Whereas such a statement imputes a kind of superiority to the speaker, there are other – perhaps more impressive – utterances in which Werther includes himself in what he perceives as the pitiful 'destiny of man'. There is, for example, the powerful moment when he observes, in fascinated horror, his own participation in the mechanisms of social life at the court. In the letter of 20 January (Book Two) he writes to Lotte:

If only you could see me, oh best of women, in the welter of distractions! How dried out my senses become! Not one moment of a full heart, not one blessed hour! Nothing! Nothing! I stand as though before a sideshow and see the little figures of men and horses passing before me, and I often wonder if it is not an optical illusion. I play along – rather, I am played like a marionette and sometimes I clasp the wooden hand of my neighbour, and then I recoil in horror.

The image of a world that has evaporated into mechanical unreality is familiar to us from twentieth-century literature: and we have to remind ourselves with what precociousness *Werther* expresses this perception of the emptiness of human affairs.

All of which, to repeat the point I made earlier, is not to convert Werther into some thinker of supremely demanding philosophical or ethical thoughts. But it does mean that whole passages of what he writes are a challenge to us: Werther's discourse is vehement in its demand that we question certain bases and presuppositions of our daily living – not least because the letter form means that we feel ourselves personally buttonholed, talked to. It is part of the rhetoric of this remarkable novel to ask us to respond to the Werther letters as both psychological and philosophical documents. If we can perform such a balancing act (and it *is* one that Goethe demands of us), we will discover the extraordinary richness that there is within this slim volume. We may even find unlooked-for riches in the title. One can translate 'Leiden' in two ways: if we render it 'sorrows', then we highlight particularly the psychological aspect. But if we render it 'sufferings' we invite the reader to see in Werther's anguish some kind of tragedy of the human spirit at its most self-aware and uncompromising.

There is a curious footnote to be added to this discussion of Werther's discourse. We know that Goethe toyed with the idea, in the late 1790s, of bringing out a series of letters concerned with a journey to Switzerland and ascribing at least some of them to Werther. The editor's preface to the first volume of the Swiss letters, which appeared in the journal *Die Horen* for 1796, was a masterly piece of equivocation:

When some years ago copies of the letters printed below were given to us, it was claimed that they had been found among Werther's papers, and it was said that he had been in Switzerland before he came to know Lotte. We never saw the originals, and we do not wish in any way to anticipate the feelings and the judgement of the reader. For, whatever the truth may be, people will surely not be able to read these few letters without sympathy.

Two points emerge from this literary–historical curiosity. First, the editor figure arouses the reader's psychological interest in Werther – do these letters sound like his handiwork, do they bear the stamp of his personality? Second, even if these letters are *not* Werther's, they will command interest and sympathy in their own right. In other words, the tentative 'sequel' (such as it was) claimed for the letters a twofold interest – as psychological evidence and as autonomous and perceptive documents on their own terms. And this may at the very least suggest that Werther's letters in the novel that bears his name were seen by Goethe himself as being valid and important on both counts.

(g) The editor

For three quarters of the text of *The Sorrows of Young Werther*, the editor ('Herausgeber') is a largely indiscernible presence. He begins the novel with a very brief, prefatory statement. There then follows a sequence of letters from Werther, in chronological order, which run from 4 May 1771 to 6 December 1772. Only thereafter does he explicitly enter the novel, almost reluctantly, bringing narrative order ('Erzählung') into the chaos of Werther's last two-and-a-half weeks. Between the editor's prefatory comment and his appearance as narrator in his own right we only notice him by virtue of the occasional footnote which he appends to Werther's letters. By far the greater part of these editorial annotations (to the letters of 26 May and 16 June of Book One, to the letter of 17 February of Book Two) serve to legitimate the documentary and com-pilatory role of the editor. When he tells us that certain proper names have been changed or omitted, he thereby contributes a note of veracity to Werther's letters: the fiction is scrupulously maintained that these are genuine documents, and in order to protect real, living people from the prying gaze of the public a certain exercise of editorial discretion has been deemed necess-ary. I have already pointed out that this veracity principle was very much part of the aesthetic convention of the epistolary novel in the eighteenth century. And throughout *Werther* the editor figure is at pains to maintain this position of dispassionate, documentary authority. Yet, as we shall see, this is by no means the only role which he fulfils. For, in the last quarter of the novel, he also assumes the role of the novel narrator who has privileged access to the inner life of his characters. This mixture of distance and empathy is characteristic of him, and it demands that we as readers react with a similar balance of detachment and complicity. In this, the editor figure is true to the function that so many of his counterparts fulfil in the epistolary novel with its twofold appeal to categories of documentary and imaginative truth. But in *Werther* that double claim is handled with unsurpassed sophistication and intelligence.

The editor introduces the novel as follows:

What I have been able to discover, by whatever means, of the story of poor Werther I have diligently put together, and I set it before you here, and I know that you will thank me for it. You cannot deny to his spirit and his character your admiration and love – nor to his fate your tears.

And you, good soul, you who feel the same promptings as he did, take comfort from his suffering, and let this little book be your friend, if you, whether from destiny's decree or from your own fault, can find no closer friend.

The opening register is one of documentary thoroughness: the editor has collected 'diligently' everything that can possibly be found that pertains to Werther's story. The second sentence immediately makes clear why Werther should have been worthy of all these labours: our 'documentary' editor asserts the kind of claim which Werther will necessarily make on us – for we will grieve over his sorry end and we will value both his particular character and the human spirit which it enshrines. The first paragraph is nothing if not forthright in its perception of Werther's worth: we are told that we will be grateful to our editor not just for his painstaking hard work but also because the object of his labours emerges as intrinsically valid in human terms – the German word 'wert[h]' denotes value, worthiness.

The second paragraph presses home the appeal. In the first

paragraph, the form of pronominal address to the reader was
the plural form 'Ihr'. Now, however, the 'you' has changed in
character: the pronoun is the intimate singular – 'du'. The
editor invokes the kind of reader who will feel a particular
kinship with Werther. And, almost by definition, it would seem,
that particularly attuned reader will both be – and feel himself
to be – solitary, an individual thrown back on his own
resources. For such a reader, the book of Werther's suffering
will provide comfort. What we hear at this point (and it is a
recurring feature of the epistolary novel) is a note of mild
didacticism. But we find ourselves wondering what kind of
didacticism is entailed. It certainly does not appear to be that of
a cautionary tale: Werther's sufferings, we are told, provide not
warning but comfort. Indeed, as the next clause makes clear, it
may be the comfort of true friendship that is provided. Yet we
must note that it is not Werther himself who provides solace,
but the book. It is difficult to be sure what the editor intends
here: at one level, his words interlock with the theme of reading
which, as we have seen, is consistently present throughout
Werther. Is the editor commending his text as the kind of
companion which Werther himself found in Homer, Ossian,
and *Emilia Galotti*? Is he thereby prefiguring the book's
success? Or is the editor invoking the book as friend precisely
because it consists of both hero and editor, of both assent and
critique, complicity and detachment? We cannot be sure.

And our uncertainty is compounded when we come to the
final clause of the editorial preface. The individual reader, who
feels the same promptings as Werther, is urged to make the
book his friend – if, because of destiny or because of his own
failings, he can find no closer one. Presumably we are meant to
detect here a note of caution, a hint that to have no close friend
other than this book is to court danger. To be thus isolated, the
editor implies, can be the result of either destiny or individual
guilt. Here we must register one of the major thematic
preoccupations of the novel (and it will sound in the very first
letter that we read). Is Werther to blame for what befalls him
(the psychological and moral issue of the novel)? Or is there a
destiny at work (the philosophical and existential theme)? We
have been urged, in the first paragraph, to shed tears for

Werther's 'fate' ('Schicksal'). Is that but a grandiose term for his sorry end – or are we to see some metaphysical agency at work? Is it the case that, in the secular, modern world, character is fate? We cannot be certain how we should answer these questions. The editor's preface is masterly in the way it initiates, but does not resolve, recurring questions to do with our relationship to the book which we have just started reading. Above all else, in that extraordinarily insidious second paragraph, it implies that the truly attuned reader of *Werther* will be the individual unsupported by corporate allegiances. Perhaps the editor implies that all of us, as readers, will be thrown back on our own resources, on our own values and judgements. This novel is a work of radical individualism: and it demands a similar radical individualism on the part of its reader. We are given the materials from which to judge. But the actual judgement will necessarily be our own and nobody else's.

I want to move forward to the moment when the editor steps into the (hitherto unbroken) sequence of letters which we have been reading; the sudden interruption is extraordinarily powerful. With no warning, we are wrenched out of the claustrophobia of Werther's letters and are obliged to stand back from him. And this comes as both a liberation and a shock (the effect is not dissimilar to that moment at the end of Kafka's *The Metamorphosis* when, after the death of the giant bed bug, we emerge into the outside world with the family who go on an outing). The editor's first utterances remind us of his documentary role and of the fact that his appearance in the novel is necessitated by the disarray of Werther's papers:

How much I would wish that enough written evidence in his own hand of our friend's last remarkable days had remained for me not to have to interrupt with narrative [Erzählung] the sequence of the letters which he left behind.

Werther is 'our friend', whereby the documentary tone softens into sympathy. The editor describes Werther's last days as 'remarkable'. But this is to understate the case: his end is not just 'merkwürdig', it is catastrophic. Our editor functions, at one level, as a documentary witness to the factual truth of what happens; but he also bears witness to Werther's end as to some

great and terrible mystery. This double stance is further
underlined in the third paragraph of his account. He promises
to tell his story 'conscientiously', to incorporate the remaining
letters at the appropriate moment – 'and not to neglect the
smallest scrap of paper'. The reason for this documentary
labour is that it is, precisely, a labour of love – 'because it is so
difficult to uncover the completely particular, true motives of
even one single event when it has occurred among people who
are not made of common clay'. We are told that Werther's
decline is intimately related to his fineness of soul and
temperament.

The editor goes on to chart – and to evaluate – that inner life.
We are clearly informed of the chaos that darkens his last days:
'the harmony of his mind was totally destroyed, an inner heat
and violence, which threw all the forces of his nature into
turmoil, had the most repulsive consequences'. Yet even such a
passage as this, which bespeaks assured narrative access to the
protagonist's inner life, is carefully buttressed with indications
of how the narrator came by his evidence – 'at least, that is what
Albert's friends say', 'they say', 'they admit'. But on the next
page, documentary caution is briefly thrown to the winds, and
the editor gives us his imaginative reconstruction of Werther's
thoughts as he trudges towards Lotte's house: '"Yes, yes," he
said to himself, with secret grindings of his teeth, "that is the
intimate, friendly, tender, generously sympathetic relationship,
the calm, lasting loyalty! It is satiety and indifference!"' We
have no grounds to doubt this account of Werther's thoughts:
we know that he becomes furiously jealous of Albert, we know
that he would be capable of such distortions of perception and
judgement. But we note that the editor has here surrendered his
documentary role in order to eavesdrop on the mind of his
character. Later in the same scene, he reports Werther's
discovery that the farmhand has committed murder: Werther
rushes over to Wahlheim to discover that the site of his idyll is
now a place of horror: 'That threshold, on which the
neighbour's children had so often played, was sullied with
blood. Love and loyalty, the loveliest of human feelings, had
changed into violence and murder.' We suspect that the second
sentence in this quotation is free indirect speech: that the

exclamation is Werther's and not the editor's. (I have already, in an earlier chapter, discussed the editor's employment of this narrative device to evoke Lotte's thoughts.) Some four paragraphs further on, however, the editor moves gently back into his documentary role. When Werther tries to defend the farmhand, we are told that his hearers, 'as one can well imagine', are unimpressed – the interpolated phrase serves to remind us that categories of probability and evidence are being invoked in this report of a scene at which the editor was not present. And when the editor quotes Werther's brief note of despairing identification with the farmhand, he does so by scrupulously observing the conjectural mode of an outsider's attempt to imagine what another person is thinking: 'how strong an impact these words *must have had* on him can be seen from the scrap of paper which was amongst his papers', which he then quotes.

The editor's account moves easily and flexibly from (on the one hand) documentary devices to (on the other) the rendering of Werther's thoughts and feelings in direct speech, indirect speech, and free indirect speech. The upshot of these seemingly abitrarily used narrative modes is, in fact, anything but chaotic or wilful. For, as the editor constantly adjusts the distance between himself and Werther's inner life, he enacts and deepens the whole dialectic of the novel. He obliges us both to stand back from Werther and view him in the context of the lives around him, as the agent in a story; and he also brings us right into Werther's mind, and makes us share in the tumult and flux of his feelings, thoughts, and perceptions.

The last page or so of the novel reports the actual suicide. We know that many of the physical details – the costume, the copy of *Emilia Galotti* on the table, the paralysed limbs, the pulse still beating, the blood on the chair, the doctor taking blood from the arm – are derived from Christian Kestner's lengthy report, in a letter to Goethe, of Jerusalem's suicide. Moreover, Goethe took not only the details: he lifted some of the formulations word for word: 'the lung rattled terribly. His end was expected'; 'of the wine he had drunk only one glass'; '*Emilia Galotti* lay open on the desk'; 'no clergyman accompanied him'. Goethe can appropriately borrow from Kestner's scrupulous report because he needs to end his novel with an account that has a documentary feel to it. In its (fictional) context, the editor's narration of the ghastly suicide is one of the most horrific scenes in the whole European novel. Werther's last letters show him envisaging a noble, elegiac death. The editor, in brutally factual mode, gives us the physical details in all their horror. This is a botched suicide, which produces hours of pain, of animal writhings ('he had rolled convulsively round the chair'). Seldom has the contrast between imagination and physical fact, between reflection and narrative event, been explored with such devastatingly laconic brutality. After the grandiloquent, impassioned prose of Werther's farewell letter ('I do not tremble to grasp the cold, terrible cup'), the editor's spare prose falls in a series of hammer-blows.

Our culture surrounds us daily with images of pain, mutilation, and violent death – on the television screen, in the newspapers, in literature. Such images need to be used sparingly – otherwise they fail to shock. Indeed, over-exposure to them can blunt our sensibilities, can anaesthetize us to horror. The editor's final page is a masterpiece of the legitimate handling of physical horror. Werther's over-heated imagination is finally silenced by this brutal death in which mind and spirit are reduced to the brains forced physically out of the skull by the impact of the bullet. He has tried to insulate himself from physical facts, from the narrative sequence of once-and-for-all events. Hence there is a rightness to the conclusion in which imaginings become deeds, in which reflection and rhapsody become action, in which physical facts, irrevocably, have the last word. Our sense of shock and pain is immense – as it should be. The editor as reporter is, aesthetically, the right witness to the terrible final events of the novel.

To sum up: in the mixture of imaginative empathy and documentary detachment, the editor in his account enacts the balance of sympathy and criticism that is central to the whole novel. He offers us both 'Erzählung' (in the sense of story-telling) and reflection (in the comments on, and re-creations of, Werther's state of mind). He asserts both the factual (quasi-documentary) and the inward (intuitively apprehended) truth-fulness of the novel. Above all, his role is central to the evaluative problem with which *Werther* confronted its con-temporary readers, and still confronts us today. Within the fiction of the novel, the editor publishes private documents (Werther's letters to his friend Wilhelm); that is to say, he makes the private public. In the second paragraph of his preface, the editor commends the 'little book' which he is compiling to the individual reader. The truly attuned 'public' for this novel will be the 'private' reader. And how that reader will judge is essentially his (private) affair. The editor will make available to us a range of evidence that extends from Werther's own self-analysis in his letters to the sober account of his catastrophic end. But the judging is left to us. One thing the editor does assert constantly is that the story we are about to hear will not leave us cold. The 'little book' will address us insistently, will demand that we take a stand.

The editor's shifting viewpoint in the last quarter of the novel makes the evaluative problem urgent but also difficult. When we enter Werther's thoughts and moods, we do so in the knowledge that they constitute one perspective, one view of the world – and not an absolute (despite all Werther's absolute claims). We may want to conclude that Werther's perspective on the world is awry, but if we do so, we may yet have to concede that this idiosyncratic view has taught us much, has enriched us imaginatively.

All this makes *Werther*, after more than two hundred years, a troubling and subversive 'little book'. It is extraordinarily modern in that it leaves us peculiarly bereft of sure vantage points – whether psychological, moral, or philosophical. The virulent responses it provoked both for and against Werther himself, both for and against the 'little book' in and through which he exists, all this confirms its undiminished ability to unsettle its readers.

(h) The reception of *Werther*

Few novels of world literature have been accorded such a spectacular reception as Goethe's *Werther*. The novel rapidly became a 'cult book'. Moreover, in recent times, *Werther* has acquired a particular centrality in academic literary discussion. One of the methods within recent literary theory is so-called 'Rezeptionsgeschichte', which seeks to understand literary history as the history of the uses to which any literary work has been put by its readers and critics over the years. *Werther* is a splendid test case, for the obvious reason that there is a full and well-documented history of readers' responses for the critic to interpret.

One problem immediately arises: the history of readers' responses tends to equate the import (and perhaps even the value) of the work of literature with its reception. Clearly the process of reception can be interesting and important in its own right. But there are occasions when particular kinds of reception tell us more about the age doing the 'receiving' than about the work or works being 'received'. Some two years ago the German Literary Archive in Marbach mounted an exhibition entitled *Classics in Dark Times*. The superb catalogue that accompanied the exhibition makes melancholy reading, for it shows the various ways in which the National Socialists pressed certain classical works of German literature into (ideological) service on their behalf. This material tells us a great deal about Germany between 1933 and 1945 – but not much about the classics themselves. Such spectacular examples give ammunition to those sceptical voices who see the history of reception as market research rather than literary scholarship.

In spite of such reservations, we must concede one point at the outset: the history of the reception of Goethe's *Werther* derives in a particular and insistent way from the character of the novel itself. As I have already stressed, *Werther* addresses the reader in no uncertain terms: that is, it makes a thematic issue of the kind of reception which it invites. And, as we shall see, the responses of readers from the last decades of the eighteenth century down to the present have in their contradictory ways interlocked with some of the profoundest issues of the novel.

I want to begin with a brief consideration of Goethe's own responses. This may seem somewhat wayward: one might assume that a writer can hardly 'receive' what he has made in the first place. But, strangely, Goethe came near to doing just that, because, as far as we know, he never read aloud from *Werther* – in the way that he did from so many of his other works. He seems almost to have shunned the work. And, even in private, he only read it rarely. When he came to revise the first version, he did so from a corrupt, printed text – neither from his manuscript, nor from the original (Weygand) text of 1774. One wonders if he was even relieved not to have the authentic version before him. He re-read *Werther* again in 1824 when he was asked (by Weygand) for a preface to a commemorative reprint fifty years after its first appearance – and his re-acquaintance with *Werther* was well-nigh catastrophic. Not, of course, that he had forgotten the novel – its huge following made that quite impossible. But it is almost as though he tried to keep it at arm's length. As we shall see, his comments express a strange interplay of affirmation and rejection. And in this he is at one with the many other commentators who, over the years, have confronted this work.

In a letter to Schönborn of June 1774 Goethe gives a brief summary of the plot of *Werther*. That summary, interestingly, concentrates not so much on the tragic love story as on the tragedy of a particular kind of, in itself, admirable sensibility:

A story . . . in which I portray a young person who, endowed with profound, pure feeling and true penetration of mind, loses himself in rhapsodic dreams, undermines himself by speculation until he finally, ravaged by the additional effect of unhappy passions and in particular by an infinite love, shoots himself in the head.

This commentary tells us little about the aesthetic character of the novel: but it does highlight the mixture of sympathy ('profound, pure feeling') and criticism ('undermines himself') with which Goethe viewed his youthful protagonist. Just over two weeks later Goethe wrote to Charlotte Kestner (the 'real life original' of Lotte) the following note:

Farewell, dear Lotte, I am sending you shortly a friend who has much in common with me, and I hope you will receive him well – he is called Werther . . .

Here one is reminded of the editor's opening injunction – 'let this little book be your friend'. In a dizzying concatenation of fiction and reality Goethe commends his fiction, on the terms of that fiction, to the one reader who is closer to the novel than any other, because she was party to the events from which it derived so immediately.

But Goethe himself was in no doubt that Werther – both the character and the book – was an explosive friend. Take, for example, the extraordinary note which he sends Frau von Stein in June 1786: 'I am correcting *Werther* and constantly find that the author did the wrong thing in not shooting himself once he had finished writing.' One notes the strangely maintained distance: Goethe refers to himself not as 'I' but as 'the author'. Moreover, what are we to make of the notion of authorial suicide? Is Goethe here saying that anybody who has written such a disturbing book as this should shoot himself? Or is he saying that anybody who has felt the kind of truth that *Werther* expresses will not be able to find the will to continue living? Implicit in the remark is both ironic detachment and self-destructive identification.

One of the questions that Goethe found himself being constantly asked was whether the story had a basis in real events. Sometimes he reacted testily. In the *Roman Elegies* (1788–9) he rejoices that he can live in Italy as a relative stranger without the ladies and gentlemen of polite society always asking him 'whether it was all precisely true'. And he continues:

> Ah how often have I cursed the foolish pages
> Which brought my youthful sorrow among people.

In such statements we hear principally irritation at the gossipy interest shown in the novel (Goethe frequently laments that it was the (factual) content and not the form which excited his readers). Caroline Sartorius reports in a letter of October 1808 how Goethe replied to a French actor's question as to the veracity of *Werther* by saying that Werther himself was two people, one of whom went under, while the other survived to write the story. This entails a familiar notion – that Werther had to perish so that Goethe might live. Caroline Sartorius's report shows us a Goethe who deals urbanely with an often posed, and unwelcome, question. But she adds a final note to her account. She reports that Goethe, having given his polished answer in French, added something in German: 'more seriously, with indescribably profound expression, he added that one could not write such a thing and escape unscathed'. What this anecdote suggests is that *Werther* issued from a wound that obstinately refused to close. And Goethe speaks of that wound in a letter to Zelter of December 1812: the occasion of the letter was the recent suicide of Zelter's stepson. Goethe writes of the terrible power of 'taedium vitae':

That every symptom of this strange, as much natural as unnatural, sickness once also surged through my soul, *Werther* can leave no one in any doubt. I still know full well what kinds of decision and effort it cost me to escape at that time from the waves of death, just as I later saved myself only with difficulty from many a shipwreck and recovered with painful slowness . . . I know I would be capable of a new *Werther* at which people's hair would stand on end even more than with the first.

The savagery of the last sentence is remarkable. It is extraordinary to hear such sentiments from a writer who is often celebrated for his Olympian transcendence of tragedy, for his serene trust in the rightness and value of the palpable world. Goethe tells Zelter that the ability – and the need – to write a new, more terrible *Werther* was very much with him, almost forty years after the appearance of the first version. Of course, this possibility is only part – and not the whole – of the man's creative sensibility. But it provides an important counterbalance to the well-nigh hagiographic assertions of Goethe's wholeness and conciliatory disposition.

Books Twelve and Thirteen of the autobiography *Poetry and Truth*, which he was working on between 1812 and 1813 (at the time of the letter to Zelter from which I have just quoted), show us a much more sovereign and detached Goethe. He looks back over the distance of many years to a youthful work which owed its prodigious resonance to the fact that it 'struck at just the right time'. But, even so, in the thirteenth book Goethe does admit something that he was often disposed to brush aside: that the interest of the public in the real basis of the novel was legitimate up to a point. He concedes that at least part of the scandal of the novel's first appearance had to do with its direct purchase on immediate events (which had been widely discussed):

On closer examination, I could not, however, resent the public's expectation. Jerusalem's fate had caused a great stir . . . Everyone was asking how it [the suicide] could have been possible, and when people heard of an unhappy love affair, all the young grew excited, and when people heard of disagreeable things that had befallen him in aristocratic circles, the middle classes grew excited, and everybody wanted to have more details. At this point there appeared in *Werther* a precise and full description in which people imagined they recognized the life and disposition of the young man. The locality and outward characters traits tallied.

This account, in view of what we know of Goethe's fascination with Jerusalem's suicide, borders on the disingenuous. But he does at least acknowledge that part of the book's timeliness had to do with its closeness to certain specific happenings, and that the public's sense of authenticated detail was not entirely wide of the mark.

The relative self-assurance with which Goethe, in *Poetry and Truth*, keeps Werther in its place is by no means sustained into his later years. On several occasions the accents of painful acknowledgement make themselves heard. In March 1816 he writes to Zelter whose youngest son had died. Again, in comforting the friend who, as before, has experienced catastrophe, Goethe invokes Werther (both the character and the book) as an appropriate witness:

A few days ago the first edition of my *Werther* came by chance into my hands, and this song, which for me had long ago faded without trace, began to sound again. One then begins to find it incomprehensible that a man has been able to endure a further forty years in a world which struck him, in his early youth, as so absurd.

Implicit in Goethe's incredulity here is a closeness between the artist and his creation: it is not just that Werther found the world absurd, Goethe, it seems, shared that view when he wrote the novel. This sense of almost umbilical linkage between the writer and his work informs the remarkable statement which

Goethe made to Eckermann in January 1824, in which he likens the novel to a living organism, calling it a 'creature which I, like the pelican, fed with the blood from my own heart'. And he goes on to give one of his most unconditional affirmations of the vehemence and truth of the novel:

It consists of nothing but rockets! Uncanny feelings come over me when I come near it, and I am afraid of experiencing again the pathological condition from which it arose.

Goethe then calls into question his own account (in *Poetry and Truth*) of the influences of English authors on himself and his generation. He now insists on the sting of specific, lived experience behind the novel:

There were individual, immediate circumstances which got under my skin and left me no peace . . . I had lived, loved, and suffered a great deal!

The Goethe who speaks here was fifty years removed from the first edition: but even at that distance he speaks of the book's rawness – and insists that it issued from, and bore the signature of, intense emotional vulnerability on his part. And then comes perhaps the most astonishing affirmation of all: 'it would be pretty bad if everybody did not have a period in his life when *Werther* strikes him as though it had been written exclusively for him'. Goethe pleads here for the universality of *Werther*: he implies more than its ability to appeal to a certain kind of temperament. Rather, he suggests that it would indicate a lack of human substance if anybody and everybody did not at some time identify with *Werther*. This is an important claim, because it has the effect of plucking Werther's experience out of the context of mere pathology – and of making it central to a phase which each man and woman must necessarily experience. We are free to conjecture what this phase might be. Adolescence suggests itself, as a period in which the discrepancy between imagined and lived experience can be particularly great. Goethe does not spell out for us what he has in mind. But he does commend the novel to universal human sympathy. Moreover, the formulation of the way this sympathy will express itself is especially telling. Goethe says that the novel will appear as though written exclusively for each reader. This is to echo the sentiments expressed at the beginning of the novel when the editor addresses the reader individually as 'du'.

In the same year as that in which the conversation with Eckermann occurred which we have just been discussing, Goethe wrote the poem 'To Werther' which now forms the first of a cycle of three poems entitled *Trilogy of Passion*. The immediate occasion that prompted the poem was that Goethe had been invited to provide a preface for a new edition of *Werther* that was to commemorate its first appearance fifty years previously. But there was more to it than this. A year earlier, Goethe, then aged seventy-four, had fallen helplessly in love with the nineteen-year-old Ulrike von Levetzow. The love which he felt was as intense as anything he had known: the grief at the parting was shattering. The figure of Werther, un-compromising to the point of self-destruction, was the true witness of Goethe's grief. Small wonder, then, that the poem 'To Werther' is one of the most heartfelt and perceptive 'prefaces' that any author ever produced to one of his own works. One salient characteristic should be noted: the ambiva-lence with which Goethe views the Werther figure. Werther is invoked in the very first line as a tearfully lamented shade, a 'vielbeweinter Schatten': the reference, of course, is to the emotional, indeed lacrymose, response which the novel elicited from the contemporary audience. Later in the poem we hear a note of unmistakable irony as Goethe counts himself among the audience that hero-worshipped Werther:

> Du lächelst, Freund, gefühlvoll, wie sich ziemt:
> Ein grässlich Scheiden machte dich berühmt;
> Wir feierten dein kläglich Missgeschick . . .

> (You smile, friend, feelingly, as is right:
> A dreadful leave-taking made you famous;
> We celebrated your piteous misfortune . . .)

The mockery can be heard in the adjectives and adverbs particularly – 'feelingly', 'dreadful', 'piteous'. In these and other intimations we hear the distance that separates the present self from Werther, the old man from the young. Yet that is only part of the truth; because the poem also suggests

that the poet's present experience confirms what Werther knew
and felt – knew and felt to the point of drawing the most radical
conclusion from his own emotional and spiritual devastation.
Hence, counterbalancing the poet's distance from the Werther
figure, we have the sense that Werther re-appears because he is
the truthful · guide to the present experiences of pain and
deprivation. Werther is not simply the alter ego: he is, for the
space of the poem, the poet's truer self. And that acknowledgement, in one authoritative couplet, overrides the perception
that Werther died in order that his creator might live. The
couplet reads:

> Zum Bleiben ich, zum Scheiden du erkoren,
> Gingst du voran – und hast nicht viel verloren.
>
> (I was destined to stay, you to part,
> You went on ahead – and you have not missed much.)

Part of the power of this couplet lies in the mixing of registers.
The first line and a half are grandiose, with the notion of destiny
('erkoren'), with the echo of Werther's biblical style in the idea
that he 'went on ahead'. Yet the final phrase is colloquial in
both tone and sentiment. The grand manner, we might say,
gives way to the bitter truth of common experience: to die
young is to miss very little. The affirmation of Werther is both
felt – and meant – to be hurtful.

The contemporary response to *Werther* was swift and violent.
I shall, in my survey, confine myself to written reactions.
But one must never forget that 'Werther fever' was a widespread and well-attested social phenomenon – silhouettes
appeared, drawings, engravings, everyday objects were de-
corated with scenes from *Werther*, and so on. It was even
rumoured that the suicide rate rose. This has not been
authenticated, as far as I am aware; but the anxiety that this
might have happened was real – as was the intense discussion of
the ethical problem of suicide to which the novel gave rise.
There was no shortage of disapproving voices. *The Gentleman's
Magazine* for 1784 records the sudden death of a Miss Glover,
and adds darkly: '*The Sorrows of Werther* were found under her
pillow; a circumstance which deserves to be known, in order, if

possible, to defeat the evil tendency of that pernicious work.'
This voice of English common sense does not want for
counterparts in Germany.

It is hardly surprising, given the character of *Werther*, that
the critical response which it provoked was polarized. The
younger generation of writers (particularly those whom we now
see as belonging to the 'Storm and Stress') – Bürger, Heinse,
Lenz, Moritz, Schubart – were unequivocal in their enthusiasm. The older generation of 'Enlightenment' writers –
Lessing, Mendelssohn, Nicolai – while often recognizing the
work's aesthetic calibre, were troubled by what they saw as its
irrationalism. And Pastor Goeze, as the self-appointed censor
of public morals, was in no doubt that this was a heinous book.

A few brief quotations will give the flavour of contemporary
critical discussion. It is striking that those who are enthusiastic
tend to adopt Werther's tone in their reviews. Schubart writes in
1774:

Here I sit, with melting heart, with a hammering in my breast, and with
eyes from which blissful pain flows in drops, and I say to you, reader,
that I have just – read? – no, devoured *The Sorrows of Young Werther*
by my beloved Göthe. I should criticize? If I could, I would have no
heart . . . Buy the book, and read it yourself! But take your heart with
you!

One notes the fiercely buttonholing address to the reader here.
There is an explicit repudiation of criticism: identification is
total. Similarly, the reviewer in the *Frankfurter gelehrte An-
zeigen* for November 1774 writes:

Happy man! You who can sympathize with Werther, who can feel that
he, in *his* circumstances, with *his* sensitive cast of mind, had to act as he
did, – I salute you as one of the select band of noble spirits!

We should also note that the enthusiastic voices are not only
effusive. In 1775 the poet J. M. R. Lenz wrote a series of letters
concerning the morality of *Werther*, letters that were not
published at the time but were passed round among friends. He
argues:

You regard it [the novel] as a subtle defence of suicide? That sounds to
me like saying that Homer's *Iliad* is a subtle encouragement to anger,

feuding, and enmity . . . The portrayal of such violent passions could be dangerous for the public? . . . Let us then examine the morality of this novel.

Lenz goes on to argue that *Werther*, in the radicalism with which it explores a particular kind of temperament, implies the necessary countervailing voice, the antidote to the poison. Blanckenburg offers a similar defence, suggesting that the truthfulness with which Werther's emotional disarray is portrayed ought to inspire us to want to help, to provide the emotional and moral correctives (he even reproaches Wilhelm for failing to respond in this way). Blanckenburg, as befits his position as the first major theoretician of the novel in Germany, is acute on the subject of the formal excellence of the novel:

How could the author better make an active figure of a man who was – and was meant to be – nothing but feeling, how could he better make all his qualities active and vivid to us than by letting this man give free reign to his heart so that it expresses itself? To whom can he do this if not to his friend? For this reason we find that the decision to cast the novel in letter form is appropriate to the man who writes them, to what he does – and should – write, and in this sense we regard this novel as one of the first to which this form completely applies.

This is a splendidly perceptive piece of literary criticism (made the more striking because Blanckenburg is, in principle, somewhat sceptical of the virtues of the epistolary novel). In respect of *Werther* he is impressed by the correlation between the form and the import of the novel. The other great analytical commentary on *Werther* comes twenty years later, in 1795, when Schiller in *On Naive and Reflective Poetry* characterizes Werther's tragedy not in terms of his individuated psychology but rather as an incomparable portrait of the reflective ('sentimentalisch') spirit:

This dangerous extreme of the reflective character has become the material for a poet in whom nature lives and moves more truly and purely than in any other, who, of modern poets, is the least removed from the sensuous truth of things. – It is interesting to see with what happy instinct everything that nourishes the reflective character is compressed together in *Werther*: impassioned, unhappy love, sensibility towards nature, religious feeling, a penchant for philosophical contemplation, and finally, to leave nothing out, the sombre, formless, melancholy Ossianic world.

In this memorable passage Schiller identifies *Werther* as the tragedy of a particular form of the modern sensibility.

As an example of the reservations felt in some quarters about *Werther* by critics who never for a moment doubted the distinction of the book, one thinks of J. J. Engel's review of 1775:

For me the character of young Werther is extremely interesting. I sympathize very much with his feelings about the destiny of mankind . . . – but otherwise Werther's feelings are, admittedly, overwrought.

Engel goes on to make the point that, while he does not believe that anybody could be seduced by the book into committing suicide, there is a dangerous imbalance in that the reasons which speak against suicide are not adequately voiced. Lessing expressed similar anxieties. In a letter of October 1774 he wonders whether a particular kind of temperamentally attuned reader might not 'easily take the poetic beauty for moral beauty and believe that he who can exert such a powerful claim on our sympathy must have been good'. Such reservations are, in view of the extraordinary power of the novel, anything but stupid or small-minded. But one hears a very different kind of voice from Pastor Goeze and his fellow guardians of public morals. That they did manage to mobilize public opinion against the novel is attested by the fact that, in Leipzig, the city council, in response to a petition from the theological faculty, made it an offence (punishable by fine) to sell copies of the novel – and also to wear the 'Werther costume'. The ban was introduced in January 1775 and remained in force until 1825. The *Freywillige Beyträge zu den Hamburgischen Nachrichten aus dem Reiche der Gelehrsamkeit* printed three reviews between 12 March and 7 April 1775 in which *Werther* is castigated for its immorality (two of these pieces are signed by Goeze, and the other – by Christian Ziegra – is unmistakably in his spirit). An extract will suffice to give the flavour:

To these writings which the author cites as visible examples of the outbreaks of depravity in our time we could add the *Sorrows* (Follies and Madness, it should be rather) *of Young Werther*, a novel which has no other purpose than to erase the scandalousness from the suicide of a young hothead, who as the result of a foolish and forbidden love and its attendant desperation comes to the conclusion that he must point a pistol at his head, and portrays this black deed as a heroic action: a novel which is not read but devoured by our young people.

The passage goes on to urge the authorities to keep a careful eye on such perverse and scandalous works.

Not all the dissenting voices are as strident as Goeze's. One of the more engaging features of the reception of *Werther* is the parodies and spoofs to which it gives rise. Friedrich Nicolai's *Joys of Young Werther* which appeared in 1775 is particularly well known. Nicolai's work does, in part, make fun of the style of Werther's letters. But what it also does is to provide an alternative ending. In Nicolai's version, Albert perceives that Werther's immoderate love threatens his very life. Accordingly, he renounces Lotte, and loads the pistols which he sends to Werther with chickens' blood. Werther is, of course, unscathed by his suicide attempt. He marries Lotte, they have several children, and, with Albert's common sense as a most useful (and welcome) corrective to Werther's inveterate emotional instability, they live happily ever after. There is an unmistakable didactic thrust to Nicolai's work: the implicit argument is that, if only somebody could have taken Werther in hand, he could have settled down to an orderly bourgeois existence. In the same year (1775) Johann August Schlettwein produced a letter which Werther is supposed to have written from beyond the grave (as we shall see later, this device will be used again, with incomparably greater distinction). In that letter Werther roundly condemns himself for the uncontrolled sensuality and loose living which led him to perdition. The point of the letter, of course, is not simply to show us a penitent Werther, but a Werther who reveals the shabby truth behind all his grandiloquent protestations of high-flown values.

By far the funniest spoof of *Werther* is Thackeray's comic ballad of 1853 which deflates Werther's stature by asserting the

sheer silliness of his emotional excesses. In the first stanza,
Thackeray invokes the most famous scene in the novel (which
gave rise to a whole number of contemporary engravings and
pictures):

> Werther had a love for Charlotte
>   Such as words could never utter,
> Would you know how first he met her?
>   She was cutting bread and butter.

The rhyme that yokes together 'never utter' with 'bread and
butter' is masterly. And the 'bread and butter' recurs with
splendid comic effect in the final stanza (which departs from the
novel, in order to celebrate Charlotte's imperturbable
domesticity):

> Charlotte, having seen his body
>   Borne before her on a shutter,
> Like a well conducted person
>   Went on cutting bread and butter.

There are two obvious reasons for the flood of *Werther*
parodies. One is that it is a novel which makes a splendid target,
because parody often derives from a delight in puncturing the
grand manner – as in the Thackeray ballad, where the spirit of
bread and butter triumphs over the heady longings of 'Empfindsamkeit'. The extreme intensity of Werther's language does,
inevitably, invite debunking. The second reason has to do with
the book's success. Not only did this mean that any satirical
reference to it would be instantly recognized: it also meant that
a parody of *Werther* could address not just the work itself but
also the kind of imagination from which the book derived and
to which it appealed. 'Werther fever' was a widespread social
phenomenon: a spoof, therefore, had both a literary and a
social target. We can get an idea of this broader social target
from a description which Friedrich Christian Laukhard gives of
a procession to Jerusalem's grave in 1776. He tells us that 'a
crowd of Wetzlar and foreign sentimentalist souls of both sexes'
gathered in the evening, sang songs, and read from *Werther*.
Laukhard continues: 'After this had happened, and people had
had a good cry and a bellow, the procession went to the

churchyard.' Somebody makes a speech in which suicide for love is condoned, and flowers are thrown on to the grave. Laukhard reports that the authorities, when they heard of a second such gathering, made it clear that no repeat performances would be tolerated; and he ends by saying that such behaviour could have been overlooked as harmless if the participants had been the unruly young, but they were, in fact, people of rank and distinction. Given this kind of public effusion, any parody of *Werther* is, by definition, also a critique of those sections of the society which greeted it with such adulation.

One might add a footnote to Laukhard's piece: he would, perhaps, not have been so surprised to find people of rank and substance involved in what he saw as pure tomfoolery had he been able to look into the future. When, in October 1808, Goethe met Napoleon at Erfurt, it emerged that the Emperor had read *Werther* seven times. Not that he was uncritical of the novel: but his dissatisfaction was directed at certain passages which he found unnatural. Goethe never tells us which passages (or passage: Goethe uses the singular in one account) Napoleon objected to. But it is intriguing to note not only that Napoleon was enthusiastic about *Werther*, but that, where he detected blemishes, they were offences against the naturalness of the novel. If even Napoleon was enthralled by *Werther*, we should perhaps be charitable towards the many lesser spirits who also succumbed.

The many conflicting responses to *Werther* are in part a tribute to its sheer eloquence. Above all, in their very divergence, the critics confirm the extraordinary balance of sympathies which the novel sustains. Much of the critical debate can be reduced to the question whether we, the readers, sympathize with Werther or not. *Werther* does provoke strong feelings – and it is meant to. Perhaps those critics are right who take a stand and come down on one side or the other of the evaluative dilemma. In the intensity of their reactions, they may be responding more truly to the novel than is the critic who offers a dispassionate assertion of the book's complexities. My own view is that the book continues to unsettle each generation of readers not only because of its explosive subject matter, but also because it demands that we constantly shift our ground when we seek to judge the novel. To talk, as I have done, of the novel's knife-edged balance is not, I hope, to domesticate it, to package it tidily. It is, rather, to seek to understand its subversive force.

The controversy which greeted the first appearance of *Werther* has not abated – nor does it show any signs of doing so. On the whole, eighteenth-century responses to *Werther* do not concern themselves with social questions as implicated in the protagonist's downfall. Yet that issue comes to play an important role in twentieth-century criticism of the novel. Perhaps the first reader to draw attention to it was Heine. Writing in 1828, he makes the point that the first generation of readers were overwhelmed by the suicide. He continues:

There is a further element in *Werther*, which captured the attention of only a small group of people – I mean the description of how young Werther is politely ejected from aristocratic society. If *Werther* had appeared in our times, this section of the book would have created a much greater stir than the whole bombshell of the pistol going off.

Marxist critics in particular have been concerned to explore the social implications of Werther's fate. Lukács in the 1930s saw Werther as someone implicitly in revolt against the constrictions of his society. Werther himself may, Lukács concedes, be unable to see the revolutionary force of his unease; but in hindsight we see him as somebody in quest of a new form of social existence. Others have dissented from this view, suggesting that Werther's individualism is bereft of any genuinely emancipatory energy because it entails a withdrawal from all engagement with the social dimension of human experience. This debate has continued to the present day. Much of its force is probably lost on those readers of *Werther* who do not have to establish its ideological acceptability before they can value it as a major work of literature. But I mention these disagreements in the Marxist camp because it seems to me that the two warring factions are enacting part of an age-old debate about the novel: how much sympathy should we have for Werther, how far should we be critical of him? Once we invest our sympathy or critique with the ideological component of whether (or not) this work of literature contributes to the necessary historical progression from feudal society via bourgeois society to a classless society, we have transposed the gulf which has always separated the 'pro' and 'contra' camps into its Marxist counterpart.

Before leaving the issue of the reception of *Werther* we will need to consider one final text – and it relates to the Marxist debate which I have outlined above. Ulrich Plenzdorf's novel *The New Sorrows of Young W.* first appeared in East Berlin in 1972. It concerns a young man, Edgar Wibeau, who is an admirable and successful apprentice in a hydraulics factory. Gradually he becomes troubled by his own conformism and, after an argument, he leaves the factory and moves from Mittenberg to East Berlin where he lives in seclusion, pursuing his own subversive enthusiasms (which include abstract painting, jazz, and jeans). He finds an old paperback edition of the novel on the lavatory, which initially fulfils a practical function as lavatory paper; but Edgar soon becomes interested in the text. He falls in love with a girl who works in a Kindergarten – he calls her Charlie. But she is engaged to somebody else. Edgar starts to work in the building trade as part of a group of painters and decorators. They are trying to develop a new spray gun. Edgar's passion for Charlie is unabated even after she is married: he often sends his friend Willi tapes on to which he records statements about his general discontent and about his feelings for Charlie (and on frequent occasions he borrows formulations from Goethe's *Werther*). Edgar continues working obsessively on the new spray gun. But his ambitions as an inventor outstrip his knowledge of electronics, and he dies of an electric shock.

Narratively, *The New Sorrows of Young W.* consists of a number of different kinds of statement: there is 'documentary' evidence (the novel opens with the newspaper reports of Edgar's death, we also hear interviews with parents and friends); but in addition we have Edgar's voice commenting on his life from beyond the grave, quoting those passages from

Werther which he records on tape for Willi. The voice from the after-life is, as we have noted, a device used by Schlettwein some two hundred years before. But the dead Edgar is by no means concerned to denounce his former self. Ironically, the 'empfindsam' theme of 'seeing one another again' (after death, that is) operates even in the modern, casual, slangy context of Edgar's self-understanding. Even allowing for the vast differences in their idiom and social setting, the relationship between Goethe's *Werther* and Plenzdorf's tale is a close one. Edgar, after initial difficulties, becomes a reader of *Werther*, just as Werther himself was an impassioned reader. When Edgar reads *Werther*, what happens to him is not dissimilar to what happens to the protagonist of Karl Philipp Moritz's *Anton Reiser* of 1786. When he reads Goethe's novel, Anton Reiser experiences something incomparably precious:

The reinforced feeling of his isolated existence, in that he conceived of himself as a being in whom heaven and earth as it were mirrored one another, meant that, proud of his humanity, he was no longer an insignificant, rejected being which he imagined himself to be in the eyes of other people.

Edgar is a similarly attuned – albeit initially reluctant – reader of *Werther*. (His other 'Bible' is J. D. Salinger's *Catcher in the Rye*.)

Of course, in Plenzdorf's novel, the whole perception of a society with its demands, norms, expectations is articulated with much greater emphasis than in Goethe's *Werther*. But common to both novels is the central concern to portray the unaccommodated self, to question whether it is not truer in and to its humanity than are the integrated existences all around it. Such a problem has, of course, a particular urgency in the German Democratic Republic, where the tenets of socialist culture tend to reject any assertion of individualism because it is seen as a bourgeois aberration.

Moreover, that Plenzdorf's hero seeks to come to terms with his own non-conformism by calling on the aid of a classic work of German literature compounds the problem: because one of the central doctrines of literary theory in the German Democratic Republic is the notion of 'Aneignung', by which is meant the process of appropriation through which a German socialist society confirms and transmits the legacy from past literatures, to which it sees itself as the legitimate heir. There is a particular urgency to this process in respect of works from the classical canon: because, so the argument runs, these works enshrine man's aspiration to attain true and full humanity, and that promise can only be redeemed by a socialist culture which has finally removed the barriers that separate individual man from his fellows.

Just as *Werther* poses a thorny problem for Marxist critics, so too Plenzdorf's novel has produced unease in literary circles in East Germany. The voices follow a predictable pattern: either we are told that Edgar's individualism is anti-social, parasitic, an evasion of the responsibilities that go with mature living; or we are told that the novel makes us attend to those energies in the self which still cry out for adequate channels of outward expression. Once again, we come back to the familiar issue: where should we stand in our evaluation of the Werther/Wibeau figure? Plenzdorf's book is as uncomfortable as is the literary ancestor which it views with strangely quizzical acknowledgement – and this is not the least of the compliments that has been paid to Goethe's novel.

There is one particular feature of the impact of *Werther* which is, as far as I am aware, unique: and that is the manifest, and publicly known closeness between the novel fiction and a real-life situation in which its author was involved. It may seem wayward to conclude a study of *Werther* by examining its genesis. On the principle of first things first, one would assume that one should begin with the genesis. But I have avoided doing this for one particular reason. *Werther*, like any work of art, must be able to stand independent of the creative process that called it into being. And any discussion of that process *before* one discusses the work itself tends, willy nilly, to lend support to the view that the novel is simply Goethe's biography writ large. In my view, the question of the genesis belongs in the consideration of the novel's reception.

I have already remarked on the fact that the eighteenth-century epistolary novel made a twofold appeal to the reader's sense of truthfulness: on the one hand, there was the claim to documentary authenticity, and on the other, the assertion that letters would be truthful in so far as they correspond to the workings of the human heart. *Werther* amply satisfies both criteria: the letters, as we have seen, convince as the expression of a particular kind of sensibility; and, as regards the 'documentary' criterion, *Werther* not only met but surpassed the expectations of its contemporary public. Rousseau begins *La nouvelle Héloïse* with a series of prefatory statements all of which are concerned with the interplay of fact and fiction in the novel. (Indeed, the second preface is a dialogue in which the Rousseau figure cleverly avoids answering his interlocutor who demands to know whether the novel consists of genuine or invented letters.) Rousseau has no doubt as to the kind of reader expectation which he is addressing. Nor has Goethe. But he meets the public desire for authentic material head on – without the coquetry of Rousseau. For Goethe's original readers, part of the scandal and attraction of *Werther* had to do with their sense that an extraordinary indiscretion had been perpetrated. In this novel, authentic material took on fictional form, private experience became public property – with a vengeance.

Goethe completed his legal studies in Strasbourg in 1771, and he then returned to Frankfurt to work in a legal practice with his father. On the advice of the latter, who felt that greater legal experience would be an advantage, Goethe went to Wetzlar where the Supreme Court ('Reichskammergericht') was situated. In the mid eighteenth century Wetzlar numbered some four thousand inhabitants, of whom nine hundred were jurists. Goethe stayed in Wetzlar from May to September 1772. There he made the acquaintance of Christian Kestner, who was secretary to the Hanoverian legation; and at a ball on 9 June 1772 he met and fell in love with Charlotte Buff who (although Goethe did not know it at the time) was engaged to Kestner. Charlotte's mother had died a year previously, and she looked after the family (which included ten younger brothers and sisters). Charlotte and Kestner were aware of Goethe's feelings, but valued his company, and it would appear that she managed, gently and skilfully, to control Goethe's emotional lability. He departed suddenly and without any farewells on 11 September 1772. He returned to Wetzlar on a brief visit from 6 to 10 November 1772: at that time there was but one topic of conversation in the small town – the recent suicide of Karl Wilhelm Jerusalem.

Jerusalem was secretary to the Brunswick legation. Relations with his superior were always strained, and at the beginning of his career in Wetzlar, he was forbidden by one Count Bassenheim to attend the more important gatherings of the social calendar. Moreover, he was in love with Elisabeth, the wife of the Palatinate Secretary Herd, but his feelings were unrequited. He shot himself, with pistols he had borrowed from Kestner, on the evening of 29 October 1772 and died the following day, at midday. During his visit to Wetzlar in November Goethe was given by Kestner an account of Jerusalem's suicide, and this was followed by a written version, which Goethe requested on 21 November. Kestner's long and detailed account is, in fact, dated 2 November, which presumably implies, if the date is accurate, that Kestner had written down the story of Jerusalem's suicide before Goethe requested it from him. At all events, when Goethe left Wetzlar on 11 November, he appears to have taken with him the original of Jerusalem's note to Kestner of 29 October 1772, in which he requested the loan of Kestner's pistols.

Goethe was, by the end of November 1772, the possessor of a great deal of documentary evidence, and it is noteworthy how precise much of that evidence was (Kestner even apologizes, at one point in his written account, for the fact that he cannot recall at which scene of *Emilia Galotti* the copy on Jerusalem's desk was open). In late 1772 Goethe met Maximiliane von La Roche in Koblenz, and was attracted to her. Just over a year later, when he met her again in Frankfurt, she was already married. Her husband, Peter Brentano, made it quite clear that he did not wish Goethe to visit his young wife. It was, it seems, partly under the impact of this experience of recurring love for a married woman that, in February 1774, Goethe began working on the first version of *Werther*. He tells us that he finished the novel in four weeks. In Book Thirteen of *Poetry and Truth* he

claims that it was the news of Jerusalem's suicide which brought
the whole plan for *Werther* into sudden focus (he uses the simile
of water, at freezing point, suddenly turning into ice when the
vessel which contains it is shaken). It is difficult to know what to
make of this statement – because the actual work on the novel
did not begin until a year-and-a-half after Jerusalem's death.
But what is clear is that the novel derives from Goethe's time
at Wetzlar, from his involvement with Charlotte Buff and
Kestner, from Jerusalem's suicide a mere six weeks after
Goethe's departure from Wetzlar, and from the repeated
experience of an attachment to a married woman (Maximiliane
Brentano).

That Goethe should draw on and combine all these experiences is not in itself particularly remarkable. But what is
remarkable is the precision and accuracy with which he copies
from authentic material. This is particularly striking in the
matter of Jerusalem's suicide: I have already pointed out that
Goethe takes not only physical details but also some actual
formulations from Kestner's account. Even the famous 'Werther costume' is borrowed from Jerusalem. And, in addition,
Goethe endows his protagonist with certain of his own
character traits. In 1772, after Goethe's arrival at Wetzlar,
Kestner wrote:

He is violent in all his emotions, but he often has a good deal of self-
control. His cast of mind is noble; so free of prejudices, he acts as the
mood takes him, without worrying whether it suits other people,
whether it is fashionable, whether conventions permit it. All constraint
is hateful to him.

He loves children and can devote himself fully to them . . . He is well
liked by children, young women, and many others.

The closeness to the Werther figure is manifest. It is also
noteworthy that, on the very evening before Goethe's sudden
departure from Wetzlar, he had discussed with friends whether
there could be a reunion after death. Later that night he wrote
to Charlotte:

I do indeed hope to return but God knows when. Lotte, how your
words touched my heart because I knew it was the last time I should see
you. Not the last time, and yet I am leaving tomorrow.

The mingling of physical (secular) notions of parting and returning with spiritual implications of a love that can bring reunion in an after-life is characteristic of Werther's letters in the hours before his suicide.

Given the extent of the overlap between fact and fiction, it is hardly surprising that part of the sensational success of the novel had to do with its reputation for being a *roman à clef*. Zimmermann in a letter to Lavater of December 1774 explores the relationship between the fictional figures and their real-life originals; a lieutenant named von Breitenbach even published a sixteen-page 'Correction to the story of young Werther'. Christian Kestner writes to his friend August von Hennings on 7 November 1774 of the points of overlap between the story and real events. He insists:

For the sake of the second part and in order to prepare for the death of Werther, he added various details to the first part which do not apply to us. Lotte, for example, did not stand – whether to Goethe or to anybody else – in the precise relationship which is there described. And we take this amiss of him, in that certain attendant circumstances are too truthful and too well known for people not to think of us.

In a letter to Goethe, Kestner protests about the Albert figure: he draws attention to the fidelity of certain external details which mean that 'people will easily think of the real one' – but he also protests at Albert's wooden inflexibility of spirit and understanding. We know that Goethe's re-working of the novel for the second version was in part aimed at meeting Kestner's objections and at checking the endless biographical speculation to which the first version had given rise.

But even the second version maintains its closeness to real-life facts and circumstances. The principle of quasi-documentary veracity which, as we have seen, was so much part of the aesthetics of the epistolary novel, operates in *Werther* not just as a component of the fiction (whereby an editor vouches for the genuineness of the letters) but also as an inalienable part both of the genesis and the reception of the novel. For generations of readers, part of the thrill of reading *Werther* was that it was not only felt, but known, to be true to life. And in our own time, the growth of the documentary novel (such as

Truman Capote's *In Cold Blood*) presupposes a similar fascination on the part of the reader with the intermingling of fact
and fiction.

As we have already noted, *Werther* is a novel in which
reading is a key theme. The moment at which the passion
between Werther and Lotte is most fully acknowledged is a
moment of reading. And the text in question, Ossian, is
particularly significant in context. We are told that Werther has
translated it into German. He has sent his translation to Lotte;
she produces it from a drawer and invites him to read it aloud to
her, which he does. And we, the readers, are obliged as it were
to look over his shoulder and read with him. Not, of course,
that Ossian is authentic material. We now know what Goethe
and his contemporaries (including the Emperor Napoleon who
was an ardent admirer of Ossian) could not have known: that
the work was a forgery. Macpherson presented himself as the
editor and translator. But he was, in fact, the author. (The
sleight-of-hand is familiar from the eighteenth-century novel.)
Macpherson claimed to have translated from the Gaelic, and
Werther translates Macpherson's 'translation'. It scarcely
matters that Werther and Lotte are moved to intense emotion
by a forgery, because the interplay of fact and fiction, the
interplay between reading, writing, and experience is so intense
that no simple act of disentangling one from another can
exorcize the complexity of the human situation which *Werther*
conveys. Much of this is captured by Thomas Mann in *Lotte in
Weimar* (1939), which concerns Lotte's visit to Goethe in 1816.
Lotte both cherishes and resents the act of artistic parasitism by
which Goethe borrowed from her experiences of forty-four
years previously and transformed them (and her) into art. In
Mann's portrayal Lotte Kestner (née Buff) resembles her
namesake in the novel in that she can neither quite forget nor
quite forgive the inroads of unconditional feeling: but she
comes to Weimar in order once again to experience the flame
that singed her – and transmuted her into 'Werther's Lotte'. It is
as Werther's Lotte that she is, on her arrival, welcomed by the
head porter of the hotel in Weimar where she takes a room. And
at the end of Thomas Mann's novel that same porter, Mager, is

delighted to be able to help 'Werther's Lotte out of Goethe's carriage.' Thomas Mann was surely right to feel that in the overlapping processes of genesis and reception, *Werther* was the supreme example of his cherished theme of the interplay of art and life. That interplay has ensured that *Werther* has gone on being read both by fictional heroes (by Anton Reiser in Karl Philipp Moritz's novel, by Roquairol in Jean Paul's *Titan*, by Plenzdorf's Edgar Wibeau), and by generations of 'real' readers from Goethe's time to our own.

It is a truism to say that the after-life of any work of literature consists in its being read. But with Goethe's *Werther* this is true with a vengeance. When we open the novel, the editor's preface tells us implicitly that the letters we are about to read are all that remains of Werther's life on earth. They are, in this sense, his after-life. And when we come to his last letters in which he, in one of the dominant motifs of Pietist literature, speaks of a life beyond the grave, we know that we hold in our hands the secular (i.e. literary) equivalent of that longed-for spiritual after-life. Just as, for Werther's sensibility, secular literature acquires the status of the sacred text, so, too, Werther's story has become, for generations of readers, a sacred text – or, to put it more modestly, a 'cult book'. Over the past two hundred years readers have reacted passionately to this 'little book'; and thereby they have contributed to the vigour of its after-life. What makes *Werther* insidious still is the fact that the process of its reception is in part the re-enactment of its theme.

Chapter 3

Conclusion: *Werther* and tragedy?

I have tried, in the foregoing pages, to give some account of the power of Goethe's *Werther*. I have suggested that we see the novel in a number of ways. We can view *Werther* as an extraordinarily convincing study in psychological decline, and we are made to participate in every current of emotion that takes Werther from the elation of the opening letters to the hideousness of the final self-destructive act. But we also see his story as one that charts the glories and the dangers of one particular kind of sensibility, a sensibility that bears the historical signature of the age of 'Empfindsamkeit'. Goethe here pushes that sensibility to its extreme conclusion. And he does so with the radicalism with which all great literature asks us to imagine 'What would happen if . . .?' But, beyond that, *Werther* also is a tragic novel in that it traces not simply the sickness of one man, not simply the potential canker at the heart of one particular cultural sensibility, but also the tragedy of the human spirit in one of its most adventurous aspects. Seen in this way, Werther's is an acute, restless, and knowing mind, and his capacity for reflection blights his ability to live: his decline is an indictment of man's disunity.

Yet we are often told that Goethe was the one writer of the modern age who resisted the dislocations and unease that self-consciousness brings in its train, who set his face against seeing tragedy as the necessary expression of the human spirit. Certainly Goethe was unflinching in his belief in the rightness and truthfulness of organic processes, of nature as the great legislator for man's experience. But he knew full well that self-consciousness was inalienably part of human – uniquely *human* – nature. He knew that men and women do not live their lives with the simple integrity of organic growth such as is displayed in a flower or a plant. He knew that we respond to stimuli from the outer world not at an unmediated, instinctual level; but that we inevitably perceive by means of certain ideas, categories, pictures, of all the images that derive from mental life.

Time and time again Goethe affirmed man's endowment with reflexive self-consciousness, although he also knew that it could disturb our allegiance to the immediate and palpable world. And in *Werther* he wrote the tragedy, not just of one flawed individual, but of the radically unaccommodated human sensibility. To see *Werther* as just the tragic exception that proves the Goethean (conciliatory) rule may be to drain it of its vehemence. In this work Goethe explores, and makes us understand, how it is possible that a sensibility that desires wholeness, totality, oneness with creation can lose its hold on the sights and sounds and shapes of the palpable world. *Werther* explores the fierce dialectic of nagging self-consciousness on the one hand and desperately willed sincerity of feeling on the other, and it counts the cost which that struggle exacts in moral and psychological terms. It presupposes a reader who is both emotionally engaged and also conscious, indeed self-conscious, in respect of the judgements which he finds himself making (hence the balance of empathy and criticism to which I have repeatedly drawn attention). *Werther* expresses unbearable human deprivation not as a contingent but as a necessary facet of man's experience. As an expression of that tragedy it has no equals in the epistolary novel of the eighteenth century: and it has had few equals in subsequent European literature.

Guide to further reading

The secondary literature devoted to eighteenth-century Germany in general and to Goethe in particular has by now become a very daunting corpus. I can only hope, in the following brief survey, to offer pointers for further reading.

On the social and cultural history of Germany in the eighteenth century the reader will find much helpful material in W.H. Bruford, *Germany in the Eighteenth Century: The Social Background of the Literary Revival*, Cambridge, 1935; Alan Menhennet, *Order and Freedom: Literature and Society in Germany from 1720 to 1805*, London, 1973; and Eda Sagarra, *A Social History of Germany 1648–1914*, London, 1977. The problems of German historiography are discussed with great verve in David Blackbourn and Geoff Eley, *The Peculiarities of German History*, Oxford, 1984. Pietism, the growth of 'Empfindsamkeit', and the interplay of religious and secular vocabularies and of public and private discourses are explored in the following works: Peter J. Brenner, *Die Krise der Selbstbehauptung*, Tübingen, 1981; Gerhart von Graevenitz, 'Innerlichkeit und Öffentlichkeit: Aspekte deutscher "bürgerlicher" Literatur im frühen achtzehnten Jahrhundert', *Deutsche Vierteljahrsschrift für Literaturwissenschaft und Geistesgeschichte* 49 (1975) Sonderheft, pp. 1*–82*, Jürgen Habermas, *Strukturwandel der Öffentlichkeit*, Neuwied and Berlin, 2nd edn, 1965; Wolf Lepenies, *Melancholie und Gesellschaft*, Frankfurt-on-Main, 1981; Herbert Schöffler, *Deutscher Geist im achtzehnten Jahrhundert*, Göttingen, 1956, especially 'Ossian: Hergang und Sinn eines grossen Betruges' (pp. 135–54) and '*Die Leiden des jungen Werther*: ihr geistesgeschichtlicher Hintergrund' (pp. 155–81).

Since 1960 there have been a number of studies on the eighteenth-century novel which have linked the growing importance of the genre to cultural and intellectual currents of the time. The following titles will be found helpful: Eva D. Becker, *Der deutsche Roman um 1780*, Stuttgart, 1963; Marion Beaujean, *Der Trivialroman in der zweiten Hälfte des achtzehnten Jahrhunderts*, Bonn, 1964; Michael Bell, *The Sentiment of Reality*, London, 1983; Maurice R. Funke, *From Saint to Psychotic: the Crisis of Human Identity in the Late Eighteenth Century*, New York, Frankfurt-on-Main and Bern, 1983; Helmut Germer, *The German Novel of Education from 1764 to 1792: A Complete Bibliography and Analysis*, Bern and Frankfurt-on-Main, 1982; Peter Uwe

Hohendahl, 'Empfindsamkeit und gesellschaftliches Bewusstsein', *Jahrbuch der deutschen Schillergesellschaft*, 16 (1972), pp. 176–207; Norbert Miller, *Der empfindsame Erzähler*, Munich, 1968; Hanns-Josef Ortheil, *Der poetische Widerstand im Roman*, Königstein/Ts., 1980; Wilhelm Vosskamp, 'Dialogische Vergegenwärtigung beim Schreiben und Lesen: Zur Poetik des Briefromans im achtzehnten Jahrhundert', *Deutsche Vierteljahrsschrift für Literaturwissenschaft und Geistesgeschichte* 45 (1971), pp. 80–116; Natascha Würzbach, *The Novel in Letters*, London, 1969.

Studies devoted to *Werther* which pay particular attention to its cultural and intellectual context include: Reinhard Assling, *Werthers Leiden: die ästhetische Rebellion der Innerlichkeit*, Frankfurt-on-Main and Bern, 1981; Richard Brinkmann, 'Goethe's *Werther* und Gottfried Arnold's *Kichen-und Ketzerhistorie*' in *Versuche zu Goethe* (Festschrift E. Heller), Heidelberg, 1976, pp. 167–89; Roger Paulin, '"Wir werden uns wieder sehn". On a Theme in *Werther*', *Publications of the English Goethe Society* 50 (1979–80), pp. 55–78. See also Nicholas Saul, 'The Motif of Baptism in Three Eighteenth-Century Novels', *German Life and Letters* 39 (1986), pp. 107–33.

Werther itself has received a great deal of critical attention. Of general studies I should mention at the outset Erich Trunz's 'Anmerkungen' in J. W. Goethe, *Werke* (Hamburger Ausgabe) volume 6, Munich, 9th edn, 1977, pp. 536–95. Trunz offers an admirable and judicious account of the novel. See also Eric A. Blackall, *Goethe and the Novel*, Ithaca and London, 1976, which contains a most thoughtful discussion of the editor figure, and H. S. Reiss, *Goethe's Novels*, London, 1979. Stefan Blessin in his *Die Romane Goethes*, Königstein/Ts., 1979 addresses particularly the social implications of the novel, and both Hans-Egon Hass, '*Werther*-Studie' in *Gestaltprobleme der Dichtung* (Festschrift G. Müller), Bonn, 1957, pp. 83–125 and Klaus Müller-Salget, 'Zur Struktur von Goethes *Werther*', *Zeitschrift für deutsche Philologie*, 100 (1981), pp. 527–44 draw attention to the aesthetic coherence of the novel. The spectrum of critical views on *Werther* is very broad. The following titles will give an idea of the different positions adopted. For a predominantly critical view of Werther which stresses his uncreativity see Ilse Graham, '*Die Leiden des jungen Werther*: A Requiem for Inwardness' in *Goethe and Lessing: The Wellsprings of Creation*, London, 1973, pp. 115–36 and 'Goethes eigner Werther', *Jahrbuch der deutschen Schillergesellschaft*, 18 (1974), pp. 268–303, and Hans Rudolf Vaget, '*Die Leiden des jungen Werthers*' in *Goethes Erzählwerk: Interpretationen* (edited by P. M. Lützeler and J. E. McLeod), Stuttgart, 1985, pp. 37–72. Werther's aggression (towards both other people and himself) is stressed by Thomas P. Saine in 'Passion and Aggression: The Meaning of Werther's Last Letter', *Orbis Litterarum*, 35 (1980), pp. 327–56. A more assenting view of Werther is taken by those critics who see him not in individual-psychological terms but rather as representative of a particular kind of spiritual energy. See for example Roland Barthes, *Fragments d'un Discours amoureux*, Paris, 1977; R. D. Miller, *The Beautiful Soul*, Harrogate, 1981; Peter Salm, 'Werther and the Sensibility of Estrangement', *German Quarterly* 46 (1973), pp. 47–55; Lionel Trilling, *Sincerity and Authenticity*, London, 1974. Anthony Thorlby, 'From What Did Goethe Save Himself in *Werther*?' in *Versuche zu Goethe* (Festschrift E. Heller), Heidelberg, 1976, pp. 150–66 suggests that *Werther* expresses a dilemma that was acutely felt by (but by no means confined to) the Romantic generation. In a suggestive article S. S. Prawer reminds us of Werther's gift for sharp (on occasion, even satirical) verbal portraiture ('Werther's People', *Publications of the English Goethe Society*, 53 (1982–3), pp. 70–97). The perspectivism of the novel is discussed by Benjamin Bennett in 'Goethe's *Werther*: Double Perspectivism and the Game of Life', *German Quarterly*, 53 (1980), pp. 63–81, which examines the narrative argument of the novel, and by Heinz Schlaffer in 'Exoterik und Esoterik in Goethes Romanen', *Goethe Jahrbuch*, 95 (1978), pp. 212–26, which has helpful comments on the relationship between Goethe's fiction and the expectations of his contemporary public. Ignace Feuerlicht provides a judicious discussion of the suicide in 'Werther's Suicide: Instinct, Reasons, Defence', *German Quarterly*, 51 (1978), pp. 476–92.

The social dimension of Werther's experience is explored in the following studies: Arnold Hirsch, '*Die Leiden des jungen Werthers*: ein bürgerliches Schicksal im absolutistischen Staat', *Études Germaniques*, 13 (1958), pp. 229–50, Gerhard Kluge, 'Die Leiden des jungen Werthers in der Residenz', *Euphorion*, 65 (1971), pp. 115–31, Georg Lukács, *Goethe und seine Zeit* in *Werke*, volume 7, Neuwied and Berlin, 1964, Peter Müller, *Zeitkritik und Utopie in Goethes 'Werther'*, Berlin, 1969; Klaus Scherpe, *Werther und Wertherwirkung*, Bad Homburg von der Höhe, 1970.

The theme of Werther's reading is treated by Richard Alewyn, '"Klopstock!"', *Euphorion*, 73 (1979), pp. 357–64, Leonard Forster, 'Werther's Reading of *Emilia Galotti*', *Publications of the English Goethe Society*, 27 (1957–8), pp. 33–45, Peter Pütz, 'Werthers Leiden an der Literatur' in *Goethe's narrative Fiction: The Irvine Goethe Symposium* (edited by W. J. Lillyman), Berlin and New York, 1983, pp. 55–68, Ralph-Rainer Wuthenow, *Im Buch die Bücher oder der Held als Leser*, Frankfurt-on-Main, 1980.

With regard to the two versions of the novel, Dieter Welz in *Der Weimarer Werther: Studien zur Sinnstruktur der zweiten Fassung des Werther-Romans*, Bonn, 1973, provides an admirably precise documentation of the linguistic changes, but his conclusions are vitiated by his determination to see the second version as symptomatic of Goethe's move from revolutionary enthusiasm to conservative acquiescence. The best recent contribution is to be found in Thomas P.

Saine, 'The Portrayal of Lotte in the Two Versions of Goethe's *Werther*', *Journal of English and Germanic Philology*, 80 (1981), pp. 54–77. Saine gives a splendidly thoughtful assessment of the 'Bauernbursch' episode and of the changing illumination of Lotte.

There are a number of publications which assemble documentary evidence concerning the reception (and genesis) of *Werther*. Trunz in the Hamburger Ausgabe, volume 6, pp. 514–36 offers a splendid array of key pronouncements. There is also the quite indispensable volume on *Die Leiden des jungen Werthers* by Kurt Rothmann in the *Erläuterungen und Dokumente* series, Reclam, Stuttgart, 1971. See also Stuart Atkins, *The Testament of 'Werther' in Poetry and Drama*, Cambridge (Mass.), 1949; Stefan Blessin, *J. W. Goethe, 'Die Leiden des jungen Werther'* (Grundlagen und Gedanken zum Verständnis erzählender Literatur), Frankfurt-on-Main, Berlin and Munich, 1985; J. W. Goethe, *Die Leiden des jungen Werther* (Editionen Klett, edited by Doris Bonz), Stuttgart, 1984; Eva Brinckschulte, *Erläuterungen zu Johann Wolfgang Goethe, 'Die Leiden des jungen Werthers'* (Königs Erläuterungen und Materialien), Hollfeld, 4th edn, 1984; Karl Hotz, *Goethes 'Werther' als Modell für kritisches Lesen*, Stuttgart, 1980: Heidrun Kaschuge, *Goethe, Plenzdorf: Die (neuen) Leiden des jungen (W.) Werthers* (Analysen und Reflexionen), Hollfeld, 5th edn, 1983; Georg Jäger, 'Die Wertherwirkung: ein rezeptionsästhetischer Modellfall' in *Historizität in Sprach-und Literaturwissenschaft* (edited by W. Müller-Seidel), Munich, 1974, pp. 389–409; Georg Jäger, *Die Leiden des alten und neuen Werther* (Hanser Literatur-Kommentare), Munich and Vienna, 1984. Eckhardt Meyer-Krentler offers a particularly thoughtful discussion of the Nicolai *Werther* parody in '"Kalte Abstraktion" gegen "versengte Einbildung": Destruktion und Restauration aufklärerischer Harmoniemodelle in Goethes *Leiden* und Nicolais *Freuden des jungen Werthers*', *Deutsche Vierteljahrsschrift für Literaturwissenschaft und Geistesgeschichte*, 56 (1982), pp. 65–91.